LE CORBUSIER REDISCOVERED

CHANDIGARH AND BEYOND

LE CORBUSIER REDISCOVERED

CHANDIGARH AND BEYOND

Edited by

Rajnish Wattas

Deepika Gandhi

NIYOGI
BOOKS

Published by
NIYOGI BOOKS
Block D, Building No. 77,
Okhla Industrial Area, Phase-I,
New Delhi-110 020, INDIA
Tel: 91-11-26816301, 26818960
Email: niyogibooks@gmail.com
Website: www.niyogibooksindia.com

Editor: K.E. Priyamvada
Design: Shashi Bhushan Prasad
Research support: Shweta Sethi, Ishita Bhatnagar and Saanya Arora

ISBN: 978-93-85285-85-1
Publication: 2018

Cover image © William J.R. Curtis; Roofscape of Assembly Building, Chandigarh
Rear cover image © VastuShilpa Foundation: Corbusier with the model of the roof
of the Assembly building
Endpapers: Front © Chandigarh Administration; Assembly building, Capitol Complex, Chandigarh
Back © Rajiv Kumar; Assembly roof in Capitol Complex, Chandigarh

Printed at: Niyogi Offset Pvt. Ltd., New Delhi, India

FOREWORD

With the recent listing of Chandigarh's Capitol Complex as a UNESCO World Heritage Site, it is opportune to both celebrate and reflect.

Historically, cities have been crucibles of civilizations. Chandigarh, a new city born in an ancient land is yet an infant in such a timeline. However, in just over sixty-five years after its inception it has carved out a unique identity of its own. It is looked up to as a symbol of modernity, energy, talent and an ideal urban model for the entire world to emulate.

Realising this significance, numerous efforts have been undertaken by the Chandigarh Administration to conserve its architectural heritage. All post-UNESCO status measures mandated in the 'Management Plan' of the Capitol Complex are being carried out in full earnest. To meet the challenges of the future in ensuring sustainable growth of the city, the Administration notified the 'Chandigarh Master Plan—2031' for its road ahead. Similarly, formation of the Chandigarh Heritage Conservation Committee and its active role ensures that all future developments are consonant with the city's unique character.

Besides the on-going expansion and renovations of the city's existing museums, recently a dedicated museum showcasing the life and contribution of Pierre Jeanneret, a close associate of Le Corbusier for the Chandigarh project, has been set up.

It's a matter of pride that with the kind support of eminent contributors from world over, and with the painstaking work put in by Professor Rajnish Wattas and Ms Deepika Gandhi editors of *Le Corbusier Rediscovered: Chandigarh and beyond,* this valuable publication has been brought out. I also commend the Administration's Department of Tourism in supporting this initiative.

With this book, the very idea of Chandigarh a 'city born in idealism' will remain alive for posterity. Its pages as they are flipped, will pass on the message of the city's ethos and its creator Le Corbusier's genius to every corner of the country and the world.

V.P. Singh Badnore
Governor Punjab & Administrator Chandigarh

CONTENTS

PREFACE

B.V. Doshi

Well-known historical cities suggest that they were conceived in the image and visions of their creators. Very often, they were saints or personalities who believed in long-lasting cultural values and the well-being of their present and future generations. Moving within those precincts, one could discover several examples, that indicate the important mandates essential for leading a harmonious life to develop societies.

Very close to such an image is the city of Jaipur, conceived and established by Maharaja Jai Singh a poet, an astronomer and a man constantly and simultaneously in touch with the galaxies. His observatories in Jaipur and his planning of Jaipur is a reminder of the virtues of discovering learning, earning, coexisting and celebrating life.

Similarly, there are our towns in South India, which radiate similar thoughts that echo a unique way of life with multiple dimensions of leading a healthy, wealthy and wise life. Such cities have been our cities of pilgrimages throbbing with life.

Soon after the partition of the country, the then Prime Minister Pandit Jawaharlal Nehru desired that Chandigarh, a new capital city of Punjab becomes a model of the 20th century inspiring the creation and evolution of our cities. In choosing Mons. Le Corbusier and his team consisting of Mons. Pierre Jeanneret, Mr Maxwell Fry and Ms Jane Drew, Nehru must have imagined that the insights they would provide to our newly Independent India would act as guidelines for future urban development. Hence for us, Chandigarh is an important model.

Historically the choice of asking Le Corbusier to lead the team meant, sowing a seed through its pioneering vision and thoughtful planning in formation of the master plan with its interconnected clusters suitable to the Indian lifestyle. That would eventually radiate the thought and concepts in creating our ideal future expansion in new rural and urban areas.

Le Corbusier opted to design the overall conceptual master plan of Chandigarh, the Capitol Complex consisting of the four important buildings in Chandigarh including the High Court, the Assembly, the Secretariat, the Governor's Palace (unbuilt) and the various monuments like the Open Hand and others to demonstrate his approaches to both planning and architecture. Perhaps, this act was very similar to our great temple builders who conceived and demonstrated the visions, thoughts and their understanding of the Indian philosophy of life and living.

I recollect reading in the newspapers, how Maxwell Fry described the importance of the foothills of the Himalayas, and how the concept of the master plan, and its values of planning and the sectors were visualised.

For Fry and Corbusier, Chandigarh was a thriving and living city. The location of the Capitol Complex and its relationship to the rest of the city was akin to that of the head with the body and the limbs. All the sectors were interconnected so as to act as if it is a human body, where the Leisure Valley would act as lungs and the streets and open spaces as veins. The city centre would thus be its heart and the Open Hand in the Capitol Complex, the spirit, which will constantly make us aware of our belief and lifestyle.

To create such a holistic and vibrant organism, the overall city was conceived with the facilities for ideal living, moving, working and cultivating body, mind and spirit. In short, Chandigarh would eventually be an ideal iconic and dynamic city of the 20th century, for India and for the world.

For Le Corbusier, the task was to express his main ideas in the Capitol Complex through great cultural diversity and paradoxes, and a way to signal how new opportunities would bring the meaning of an ideal habitat where both, contemporary and future values are integrated. This was an opportunity to positively exploit the constraints of the Indian economy, adoption of new technology, reinterpret ways of her diverse culture and give the population a model of how a great ancient past can be reformed into an ideal future.

Incidentally in Le Corbusier's life too, this phase of building in India was new and his initial mode of communication with his staff and workers was only through hand, eye movements, gestures and sketches. Often in his talks, speeches and drawings Le Corbusier mentioned about the hot, scorching summer sun, the cool winter months and the torrential rainy season. They appealed to him as the major concerns and became potentials for his new expression in planning and design.

I remember Le Corbusier's insistence on incorporating an understanding of everything. He insisted on expressing his ideas of 'Pact with Nature'. Perhaps the large plain at the Shivalik foothills was such a sacred site, that the hills, though far away, would yet provide wiser counsel, eternity and reverence for the citizens of the city from everyday political intrigue.

He made sketches of his first impressions of India and the Himalayas, the site of the Capitol Complex and the blue sky full of large soaring birds. He felt and sensed the need for air circulation and its connectedness to the open sky. In another drawing he expressed the beauty, grace and dignity of a woman, on her waist a child against the backdrop of the vast open space.

For him, India appeared to be an open field of both spiritual and physical experiences, perhaps his theory of distinct routes of movement which also emphasised the importance of walkable neighbourhoods at varied scales linking all the internal activities including socio-economic, cultural and recreational facilities.

On the other hand for him the vast unemployed labour, low technology, scarcity of material and Indian ways of perceiving space, light, form, materials, etc., meant conceiving new ways of understanding architecture. He attempted to develop multiple yet simple structural systems to build unexpected structural systems around local technologies and locally available materials. For him this was a positive way to manipulate the vagaries of extreme climate. As a result he and his colleagues over time upgraded local technology, trained available manpower and conceived new ways of planning of open spaces with minimum enclosures to allow cross ventilation and diffused light.

Since human behaviour usually senses and formulates configurations, understanding of scales of spaces, their multiple uses and relationships is a need in order to provide open-ended solutions. It is further enhanced by their exposure to natural or artificial light and connecting natural elements such as sky, trees and water with the activities.

His sketches of planning and designs of his housing clusters fostered integration of nature and lifestyle to create private and public spaces. One can notice that by simultaneously working on totally different scales, he showed his remarkable ability of expressing and experiencing architecture, challenging the traditional mode of building. Thus he intended to incorporate in the Sector plan his notions of private to public, timebound to timeless, singular contact to plural aspirations, from personal to societal ways of built forms and open spaces.

His use of *beton-brut* with local crafts, exploited shadows with patterns through which one could feel the breeze, patina of monsoon rains, and need for shade and ventilation.

As always he fused the engineer and the artist in him and demonstrated his concerns about buildings for the masses and availability of resources to all. He proposed alternative hybrid micro-level devices and new methods of saving energy connected to the Indian cultural ethos. He noted in his diaries his understanding of the essence of life in India, and tried to respond to her culturally rich and accessible lifestyle.

Rather than finite solutions he proposed flexible alternatives such as layered systems. He admired the way Indians use their clothing or outdoors spaces to suit seasons. Open-endedness or finite, he proposed greater permeability and multiple uses with hybrid technology. His search for greater value in juxtaposing counter points or apparent paradoxes can be seen in the design of the High Court and Assembly.

Le Corbusier, through illustrations in the enamel door in the Assembly portico tells us that we as architects, must regard and incorporate universal laws in our design to achieve peace and prosperity. The birds, the bull, the shells, the serpent, the tortoise, the fish, etc., depicted on the door are diverse examples of universally guided life and they tell their own story of co-existence. He advises us to search for our balance and wisdom to live a revered life. More importantly through this understanding, he wants us to remember, the symbols that he created in the Capitol Complex along with the Tower of Shadows and the other diagrams. For me his buildings reflect a representation very similar to that of the great artists of the Renaissance.

There are many hidden lessons. They are the seeds of great architectural meaning. So here are a few thoughts:

Chandigarh is located on a wonderful site viewing the Himalayas. We should somehow preserve this very special asset, for which, it is essential to build little and with perhaps high density but low-rise settlements, where life will still be quite peaceful if it is full of trees and many sacred institutions. This way the *darshan* of the sacred Himalayas is possible.

In all our decisions we must give priority to our lifestyle both traditional, contemporary and future, but only through providing natural ways to preserve energy and resources. We need to create settlements to add greater cohesion and vibrancy to life.

The hierarchy of seven types of roads (7 Vs) that are part of Chandigarh's circulation system suggest that every function and location can be peaceful so we need to create clusters of well-connected settlements with all socio-cultural facilities which enhance both human and technological virtues.

We realise that the hierarchies of lifestyle have their virtues and economies of scale. If we consider land as sacred and design according to the various types of relationships, the combined effect would save movements, add pauses and avoid atmospheric or time pollution.

As depicted in the portico of the Assembly, all life is ruled by our universal cycles of the sun, rains, wind and earth.

We should create land-uses which are mixed and which save energies at all levels and we as Indians too have our own identity and we should give our buildings a unique expression so that at all levels frugality, cooperation, togetherness, tolerance, sharing and reverence is celebrated. Our lifestyles are diverse, so are our abilities to sustain and enhance lifestyles. Let our plans and atmospheres demonstrate that.

And lastly, as Le Corbusier's buildings demonstrate that all accesses, dialogues are open and lead to sacred values, we too should design unique appropriate, time and energy saving built-form that we call architecture.

Remember, all cities are living organisms and they should be treated as part of us as beings. Chandigarh has this chance to constantly upgrade and demonstrate its unique position in India and the world around.

Le Corbusier observed that the Indian communities live in groups, *mohallas*, a complex social fabric which fosters interaction. Indians like to live as much outdoors as indoors; use private and public gardens and lots of open shaded areas. In addition there is socio-economic interdependence. And as a result the citizens as well as visitors adore being in Chandigarh and rejoice peacefully without vehicular disturbance. There is a planned hierarchy, which is unique.

Leaving aside Chandigarh's iconic structures like the Capitol, Museum and Art gallery, Lake Club, schools of art and architecture, most of the city's remaining visible fabric and builtform in the first phase comprising public buildings like schools, colleges, hospitals, government offices, etc., and government housing for its employees were designed by Pierre Jeanneret, Maxwell Fry, Jane Drew and their Indian colleagues. These simple, austere brick and stone structures built with shoe-string budgets along with Corbusier's grand monumental work influenced the post-Independence generation of young Indians—thus establishing what one may call a popular pan-India 'Chandigarh school of architecture'. Notwithstanding numerous innovations in materials and technologies this mode remains a predominant simple, affordable way of architectural expression and construction.

In case of Chandigarh, a relatively young city, one needs to be aware that over time it too can lose the virtues enshrined in its original mandate.

Luckily it has the most powerful, revolutionary and exemplary iconic buildings. There are many lessons which we can still emulate and filter new concepts.

However, it must plan immediately—as the recently notified Master Plan 2031 attempts to—for its growing population, ingress of cars and impediments to pedestrian and cyclist movement. Corbusier had foreseen such an expansion in the future and therefore left conceptual sketches for Chandigarh's 're-densification'. Satellite towns of Mohali, Panchkula, Zirakpur, Mullanpur and others are choking the city in a chaotic urban gridlock, They threaten to subvert the very spirit, the noble idea, the cherished human values that Le Corbusier conceived of in Chandigarh.

The city authorities and its citizens therefore must safeguard this national or rather global heritage.

There are many cities in India which are constantly getting expanded. Often one notices that our cities of the past that endeavoured to create great heritage, eventually got overshadowed by the onslaught of new developments. Currently all Indian cities are losing their inner strength and virtues.

In the present scenario where the cities are ever growing, it is upon us to decide how the future cities would look like. We have the choice either to configure spaces, forms and their relationship to nature, making the cities as unique as Chandigarh or to neglect the principles laid down by our predecessors.

This book *Le Corbusier Rediscovered: Chandigarh and beyond* is an extension of the very noble idea of the city itself. It bravely, diligently brings together in a rare anthology, contributions by numerous brilliant and legendary minds—that both celebrate and address various aspects of the values enshrined in the spirit of the Chandigarh project. Such a documentation and collection of expert voices, carries forward the discourse initiated by the idea of Chandigarh.

KEYNOTE

William J.R. Curtis

Thank you very much for the invitation to be here with you all for this great commemorative event marking the 50th anniversary of the death of Le Corbusier. To give the keynote address on this occasion and in this precise place, the centre of the Capitol of Chandigarh, has special personal meaning to me, as I shall later explain. I am honoured to be on this platform in such elevated company and among old friends. I salute both officials and anonymous citizens of Chandigarh at all levels of society for contributing to the restorative work on the Capitol and for organizing such a splendid celebration.

I would like to dedicate these thoughts on the significance of Chandigarh to a very dear friend, P.L.Varma, the former Chief Engineer of the Punjab, who was in so many ways the animating spirit of the Chandigarh project. In effect he was Le Corbusier's client for this vast endeavour. Without clients of stature, major architectural achievements are much harder to achieve. Varma and I established a friendship here in 1983 and we had an extremely intense dialogue for several years of continual visits and exchanges. My wife Catherine and I were often invited to dine by Varma and his wife in their house in Chandigarh. He was a remarkable person. He was a rather aloof and patrician individual, which was probably necessary in order to steer things through. He saw the big picture and had no time for the trivial machinations of what he called 'Lilliputian politics'. He fought for the Sukhna Lake. I think we can all thank Varma for the lake and for so much else, but he was also a storehouse of reflection and information about the background history and eventual development of Chandigarh.

Varma referred quite often to the upheaval of Partition in 1948, which he and his family experienced first-hand as they had to leave behind their home and their past in what became Pakistan. Chandigarh is a city founded in large part for refugees. It is a city of national foundation and of personal re-foundation. There were all the individual histories of leaving Lahore with only suitcases, of the massacres that took place, of people living in tents outside of Delhi. But this also amounted to a collective crisis on a huge scale. So Chandigarh was, yes, one of the foundation documents of the new nation, the independent and secular Republic of India. Pandit Nehru could have treated this as a provincial operation, but he did not. He treated it as a national operation. Partly this had to do with geopolitics and holding the northern territories, as things were loose and borders were very fragile; these were strategic considerations. But Chandigarh was also founded to provide a home for those who needed to resettle their lives and start afresh. In turn of course it was to give a new administrative capital to the Indian portion of the newly divided Punjab, as the old capital, Lahore, had been left on the Pakistani side.

In the history of architecture it is extraordinary how many key monuments have grown out of major social disasters and political upheavals. Hagia Sophia, the great 6th century church in Constantinople, came about after massive riots, when the state was almost ripped apart. It was an assertion of divine imperial rule. The role of the monument is to idealise institutions. It does not portray things the way they are, it portrays things the way they ought to be. Le Corbusier knew that this was the role of architecture here on the Capitol. Whatever the program stated concerning parliament, law, etc. he saw through it to the deeper meaning. With this intention of founding a new city he immediately saw an opportunity to insert many of his key doctrines to do with green cities, to do with the so called 'essential joys' of space, light, greenery, to do with circulation, all the things that were basic to his urbanism. At the same time it was an opportunity to concentrate on something which had been elusive in his life, monumentality. The architect who designed the project for the League of Nations in 1927 for the Lake side in Geneva, but lost the

Facing page:
P.L. Varma (former Chief Engineer of Punjab), Mrs Varma and the writer in Chandigarh in 1983.
© Catherine Curtis, 1983

commission, the architect who designed the Mundaneum in 1928, but failed to construct it, really had monumentality at the heart of him. The problem was that he never had the opportunity to construct monuments until the Chandigarh project came along.

What a curious turn of events then that it was in India, poor materially but culturally rich, and not in relatively rich Europe or in very rich America, that he realised this dream. Another great monument of modern architecture was created soon after and also out of a divisive political situation, the Assembly Complex by Louis Kahn in Dhaka, Bangladesh, once East Pakistan, and before Partition, an integral part of Bengal. These two major figures of modern architecture, Le Corbusier and Kahn, were in their mid-sixties, the age I am now more or less, when they came to the sub-continent. And they discovered new dimensions of themselves by being here. Le Corbusier found many resonances in India and the Indians took to him. My friend Balkrishna Doshi, who unfortunately cannot be with us today, always felt this other dimension with Le Corbusier. Behind the severe façade with the horn-rimmed spectacles, there was this other person, a man of deep spiritual insight. Doshi told me, 'we thought of him as a sort of a guru, we realised he could see further, beyond the surface of things.'

All this is corroborated by the extraordinary discussions I used to have with Varma. Le Corbusier had a rather amateur interest in Hindu philosophy and Varma guided him in a way. Varma recounted his many conversations with Le Corbusier. One day Le Corbusier said, 'Varma, do you know what my High Court building is all about?' Naturally Varma replied, 'No Le Corbusier, what is it all about?' And the architect replied, 'It is about the majesty, the strength, and the shelter of the law.' I think that this reveals something about the way Le Corbusier invented projects. There is a generating idea, an underlying myth, an image. In Chandigarh there is the theme throughout all the buildings of the protective parasol, it is a leitmotif, a type. This is Le Corbusier's way of thinking. He comes into a new situation with a very rich baggage of forms, and ideas and types, but he has his eyes open for something that helps to spark invention in each new situation; and in the Indian situation he sought a device that could protect from sun and rain while also supplying the potential of an appropriate institutional symbolism for democratic institutions.

On his first trips to India in the early 1950s Le Corbusier was hugely impressed by the power of the monsoons. In his pocket sketchbook he did drawings showing parasol roofs in the form of huge gutters sluicing water off at each end. There is the germ here of the porticoes of the Parliament and High Court. On his first visit in Delhi he sketched verandas and the entrance pavilion to the Tomb of Humayun. He also visited the Jantar Mantar, the astronomical devices designed in the early 18th century by Jai Singh (later he would appreciate the ones in Jaipur). After seeing these cosmic instruments resembling huge abstract sculptures, he wrote in his notebook: 'The astronomical instruments of Delhi...They point the way: re-link men to the cosmos....Exact adaptation of forms and organisms to the sun, to the rains, to the air, etc...this buries Vignola'. For Le Corbusier, the 16th century Renaissance architect and classical theorist, Vignola represented the worst of academicism. Note the role of direct observation in Le Corbusier's creative procedure: his mind was always ticking over, his eye latching onto diverse things. I have always been interested in this part of Corbusier. The part that like Leonardo da Vinci observes a crack in the wall, or a bird flying or a hand or a tree and transforms it through magic into the forms of his universe. The Open Hand did not really start in Chandigarh. It probably started when he was a young man sketching trees and hands. His images transform, and re-transform and then transform again into something else in a series of metamorphoses. Ideas interact with forms; forms interact with ideas.

So for me it is a very personal matter to be standing here on the Capitol of Chandigarh at this symbolic event because this place has been so important in my life. Indeed India itself has played a central role. I first came here in May 1980. I did not know anybody in India. I was on my way between Australia and England, but I had decided to stop in India for two or three weeks and particularly wanted to see Fatehpur Sikri, but also, of course, Chandigarh. Actually I went to the Mughal monuments first in Delhi and in and around Agra and was blown away by them, especially the Tomb of Humayum. I eventually took a bus from the north bus station in Delhi, came rolling up here to Chandigarh in the extreme heat and found a little hotel. But I did have a letter of introduction from Peter Johnson, the Australian architect, to Aditya Prakash who was Director of the Chandigarh School of Architecture in those days and who had been an architect in the Le Corbusier/Pierre Jeanneret team as well. I phoned him up, he said, 'come and have tea tomorrow morning' and I did. He arranged a chit at half-an-hour's notice and this permitted me to go all over the buildings on the Capitol. I spent an exhausting day clambering all over the roofs of the Assembly taking photographs, went to the yacht club to cool off, then went to drinks on the parched lawn of Aditya's home, and finally took the train back to Delhi. I was transformed by this experience of Chandigarh, just as I was by that of Fatehpur Sikri.

For me architecture is something visceral, direct, which moves me profoundly. It touches the mind, the body, the senses and the memory. My books on architecture attempt to reconstruct past contexts and the intentions behind works: both the guiding ideas and the world view. But buildings have their own presence and continue to speak to us directly as the materialisation of architectural thoughts, and this aura I try to capture as well, partly through texts, partly through photographs. Powerful architecture cuts across time and continues to move us by its own means. When I walked up here onto the Capitol this evening and saw the monuments again in this soft October evening light with the raking shadows on the forms and materials, I was quite simply knocked sideways. I recalled Le Corbusier's definition of architecture in his famous book of 1923, *Vers une architecture* (Towards an Architecture): 'Architecture is the magnificent, correct and knowledgeable play of volumes assembled under light'. So much for the direct impact of the forms: as to the meaning behind them, that is the principal subject of my talk tomorrow.

Over the years I got more and more involved in India in many ways and with diverse people, some here present as friends or colleagues. I was also involved in writing texts, including for example, an introduction to a book on Raj Rewal (1986) and an entire book on the work of Doshi: *Balkrishna Doshi: an Architecture for India* (1988). I also became deeply interested in the history of ancient architecture, trekking across the countryside of deepest India, and visiting places such as Aihole or Pattadakal in search of the roots of the Hindu temple, or Sanchi to comprehend Buddhist forms and symbolism. I was accompanied on all these treks by my wife Catherine and the conditions were sometimes tough. We moved around rural regions on single gauge railways, on horse-drawn tongas, by buffalo cart, or else by walking considerable distances. I gradually realised that India is a place that rethinks its own architectural history, every so often, even on a grand scale. Fatehpur Sikri, for example, absorbed and transformed ideas from diverse earlier

Facing page:
Labourers in Capitol Complex, Chandigarh, with the Secretariat and Assembly in the background
© William J.R. Curtis, 2014

traditions in a new synthesis mirroring Akbar's inclusive model of imperial rule. In a sense, the Capitol in Chandigarh does this too but with a democratic and inclusive imperative for a post colonial, secular nation state. It is a sort of political and cosmic landscape, full of resonances with great things from the past. You find the open hall or Diwan-i-am of the Mughal justice system transformed into a language of reinforced concrete in the High Court. The unbuilt Governor's palace is a subtle reinterpretation of the Diwan-i-khas of Fatehpur Sikri. The parasol with its upturned crescent motif, is a dome turned upside down, an anti-imperialist gesture that is linked to the sky rather like an abstract version of the Open Hand. It is a reinvented *chattri* as well, even an umbrella that comes from the Buddhist system of symbolism. Le Corbusier had this amazing ability to see through history to the basic types and then to pull them forward into modernity and transform them.

Among my many dialogues over the years there were private ones, of course, but there were also public events. There was a wonderful congress here actually, in early 1999, 'Chandigarh, 50 Years of the Idea'. This was initiated by the then President of the country, K.R. Narayanan, who gave the most intelligent speech I have ever heard by a politician on architecture and urbanism and why they matter to a society. With all due respect I certainly cannot remember anybody in the British Parliament achieving that and certainly not in the Chambre des Députés in Paris: maybe in the Swiss Parliament in Berne? The French Ambassador came and recalled that it had been the French Government that supplied the financing for the enamel door to the Assembly building. Charles Correa, one of the organisers, achieved an overnight miracle by having a replica of the Governor's Palace erected in temporary materials of wood and fabric. Interventions were made by architects and scholars from all over the world. I remember being on the first panel with Achyut Kanvinde, Peter Smithson and Denys Lasdun, alas now all gone. Lasdun, himself a master of monumentality (the National Theatre in London) was seeing these great works by Le Corbusier for the first time and was astounded. Later I took him and his wife Susan to the Jain Temple at Ranakpur with its cascading strata and Denys said: 'You see William, it has all been done before'.

Over the years I have experienced Chandigarh in many moods and atmospheres and have gauged the rapid social and economic changes.

When I first went up to the Capitol in May 1980 I was in a scooter rickshaw and counted three cars on the main axial road. Today there are traffic jams! I recall the political crises of the early to mid-eighties with the fears of attacks on buses and the like. I remember meeting with Vikram Prakash (son of Aditya) and three of his fellow students on the ramp at the centre of the Capitol in 1983 and founding with them a sort of discussion group on architecture. Then there were the spring evenings with the smell of blossoms, or the extraordinary occasions when one would see the sun go down and the moon come up simultaneously. In the early days, villagers and cattle wandered across the Capitol, children played in the tanks, and the Open Hand lay in fragments in the grass. I have known Chandigarh in cold winter fog and in extreme summer heat. So here I am again in an autumn that has clearly gained from intensive rainfall to judge by the rich vegetation in the countryside of the Punjab. The strong architectural forms poking out of the greenery, cross lit just before sunset, produce a powerful and unforgettable effect. I am also a photographer and so I register my reactions towards architecture, beyond the word, through the image. Tomorrow I shall talk more about this because I realise that photography is part of our programme here too.

In the end, Le Corbusier remains an enigma. I think of a sketch he made in Egypt on one of his stopovers on the way to India. It shows the pyramids of Giza with the Sphinx in the foreground. Did he identify with the famous 'riddle of the Sphinx'? The further I go with Le Corbusier, the more I realise there are hidden depths. In my book *Le Corbusier: Ideas and Forms* (2nd edition, 2015), which is being presented on this platform this evening, there is a very full chapter on Chandigarh and another on Ahmedabad. This book developed out of an earlier edition (1986) but I have modified it hugely, it actually has five new chapters in all. One delves into the intentions, but there is always a dimension in great architecture that escapes analysis. Buildings evolve over time as the context shifts. Some wonderful things have been done recently to try and make the Capitol more part of the life of the city. We all know this is an issue, and that it has been an issue for a long time. The space of the Capitol has been a contested territory and it started almost as soon as the cement was dry with the creation of Haryana and the subsequent division of buildings and functions. Then there are all the security issues. I was here at the time that Sikh separatists wanted to transform Chandigarh into the capital of a separate state of Khalistan. I recall the massacre in the Amritsar golden temple and the assassination of Prime Minister Indira Gandhi. I know the story quite well.

Over time this extraordinary ensemble of buildings on the Capitol has entered the political consciousness of the nation. Chandigarh was supposed to embody democratic and secular values beyond issues of ethnicity, caste and creed. Le Corbusier understood that perfectly well, but it did not stop him looking for a certain quality of the sacred in his monuments. When you go into the Assembly or Parliament building with its amazing hall of columns, the black soffit floating in light, you are in the presence of an epic work of architecture. It is a celebration of the idea of 'understanding'—an architectural image which suggests a shared soffit under which one may come to an agreement. At the same time this space recalls hypostyle halls in the history of architecture, even those in ancient Indian temples. Le Corbusier understood these basic archetypes in the history of architecture and transformed them. You pass on into the Assembly chamber with its great funnel and the light breaks in from above. In Le Corbusier's original idea, there was supposed to be a ray of light touching a small column of Ashoka, marking the opening of parliament. The idea recalls the Pantheon in Rome or even solar temples in India. Le Corbusier evoked ideas of regeneration in relationship to nature and to the cosmic rhythms. 'Man', he claimed, needed to be reminded that he is 'a son of the sun'.

So much for the past: what now about the future? I was here a year and a half ago and was quite disturbed by the state of things, by the degradation of some of the spaces and buildings and by the shabby and abandoned state of the Capitol space itself. I was even more disturbed by the state of things in Ahmedabad where I saw how vulnerable Le Corbusier's and Louis Khan's buildings are to developers seeking profits on land in smash and grab capitalism. The pressure on real estate in India is enormous and four years ago there was actually a full scale attempt to demolish Le Corbusier's Millowner's Association Building, as it occupies a prime riverside site overlooking the Sabarmati. In a state of shock at the lack of local reaction I decided that the time had come to blow the whistle. I have gone into action on this issue in the press, first of all in England (the *Architectural Review*) then in the *Times of India*, Chandigarh edition. Then there was a major piece in *Architecture + Design*, thank you Suneet Paul the Editor, here present. In this constructed dialogue between

Facing page:
Secretariat, Chandigarh,
access ramp
© William J.R. Curtis, 2014

William J.R. Curtis and an 'unknown Indian' (myself!) entitled 'Protecting Modern Masterpieces in India', I put the whole argument for the following: I said 'Look, it's great to get the UNESCO, it's wonderful as a kind of cherry on the cake but that does not guarantee protection, it gives prestige. So what is needed is a change in the heritage laws in India, a new act of Parliament at the national level. Nothing less will do.'

At the moment 'heritage' is defined in India as being more than 100 years old. But the Parliament or Assembly Building in Chandigarh is a future Taj Mahal or a future Fatehpur Sikri. With the ensemble of the Capitol as a whole it will become national patrimony, part of collective memory, and it needs protection now. How tragic if it was handed on to future generations in the great nation of India in some way damaged or sullied. The same goes for the wider space around the Capitol and its relation to the foothills of the Himalayas. If corrupt people start building 18 storey apartment buildings pretending they are farms and breaking all the rules, we are in trouble. So the present atmosphere of boom laissez-faire economics is generating a certain kind of wealth in India and no one wants to deny people wealth but it is also destroying a commonwealth and impoverishing public space everywhere. Raj Rewal brought this up already and I am bringing it up in yet another form. So I believe that thought has to be given by the judiciary to updating what we mean by heritage and re-defining it in law. Only then will modern masterpieces in India be protected. This can only help the UNESCO protection process, because it would constitute one more safeguard.

Wonderful things have been done to clean things up since I was last here and I am grateful for that. I was so pleased at long last to find no fence cutting across the Capitol. It took me back to the days where I used to photograph the whole width of these buildings in dialogue. But let me now make a slightly spicy remark. I do not know if anything has been done to restore the great hall of columns in the Assembly to its original state. When I was there last, I was astonished to discover that the slender concrete columns had wooden ankle socks rising to about two meters. There were sort of restaurant screens cutting across the space and a stone floor worthy of a 2 star hotel! This will not do. Come on, you wouldn't go to Taj Mahal and start putting green tiles in one place, knocking it about in another, and sprucing it up with vulgar and inappropriate additions. This is world patrimony, this is universal patrimony. So with all respect to the politicians in place, you are temporary custodians my dear friends of something that belongs to all of us in the future and to future generations, so I request more thought and more restorative action on that front.

But anyway, the spirit here is not to carp and complain. We are here to celebrate an extraordinary place, an extraordinary achievement. Then there is the question of completing or not completing the Capitol. This is a really tricky issue. You will know there was a project by Le Corbusier for the Governor's Palace. But what you have to realise is that there was not just one: there were three versions of the same thing but at different scales. So if we are talking about building the Governor's Palace, which one is the correct version? Then there was that substitute project of Le Corbusier for a 'Museum of Knowledge'. In my view this is certainly the worst project Le Corbusier ever designed, which was shoved in as a possible alternative. The Governor's Palace is a great project, but does anybody really know how to build it? Do they really know how to do the details of such a building? Do they really know how to do the valleys and waterbodies in front of the building which are evoked only in rough sketches and without precise drawings? It is really a risky business to proceed on such shaky grounds. It is in any case risky to build posthumously as one may judge from the example of the Church at Firminy completed years after Le Corbusier's death. To me this is a fake, it is not a true Le Corbusier building. Even when you have drawings there is the fact that Le Corbusier often changed things on site. Even the very process of building changes with time. So there are many tricky questions around the issue of building the Governor's Palace.

But there are surely other moves that can be made up here by using landscaping to help resolve the space beyond the limits of the Capitol. Needed perhaps is a green buffer zone of mounds and valleys to protect against real estate development to the north east. One should think seriously about realising a version of Le Corbusier's formal grid garden of trees shown in the overall plans as being beyond the limit of the Capitol. This could even be accessed from underground by means of an extra stop on the metro but without disturbing the Capitol itself and while maintaining security. So there are a lot of things you can do with soil and vegetation. Soil you can retract, if you think it's not okay you pull it out. If you erect whole Governor's Palace and if it actually does not work, well then you really have a hot potato politically! So I would say, develop very slowly on this issue, think it through. It is obvious that this place is without a head but if a building goes there, it has to have a real function. In 1999 after I came here I wrote an article in the Japanese journal *A+U* arguing that the Capitol should be treated as universal patrimony of humanity and saying that if somebody does proceed with the idea for the Governor's Palace they should have a viable use for it.

If one follows this line of speculation one would say that such an institution ought to be ambitious in its aims: not just local, not just national, but also international, even universal in its range. Raj Rewal and I talked recently about the idea of a Centre of Architecture. It could go even further and be a Centre for the Study of Architecture, Urbanism and Nature and what these mean to each other in a rapidly changing world. This could be a citizen's forum of course but it could also bring people, ideas and exhibitions from the rest of the world. India desperately needs a proper centre of this kind. In any event, the Capitol has to be reclaimed by the citizens of Chandigarh and good moves have been made by the current administration in that direction. Many wonderful things could happen up here and even in the valley under the Open Hand, dance festivals for example. Le Corbusier himself never thought of the Capitol as a sort of Piazza San Marco thronging with people. His drawings show social assemblies on the roof terraces, which is really a problem I admit. But when you go up on the roof of the Parliament or the Secretariat, you have that incredible view of the landscape. He was thinking of the roofs as social spaces, communal theatres, but I do not think it likely that his vision will be realised. So with the Chandigarh Capitol we are in the presence of an incomplete masterpiece. Even so, it resonates, speaks to us with great directness across time. For surely one of the roles of the monument is to transcend time, allowing new interpretations and new meanings.

The Open Hand was always rather vague in its significance. Le Corbusier used phrases such as 'open to give, open to receive'. In his mind, India was supposed somehow to bypass the tensions of the first machine age and to establish a more satisfactory relationship with nature in a post colonial world order. Talk about a utopian fiction! Le Corbusier responded to Nehru's socialist and progressive vision for India, but preserved a fascination with Gandhi's notions of an enriching rural base. He even latched onto Nehru's notion of a 'third world' that would be non-aligned with either American led capitalism or Soviet led communism.

Le Corbusier's utopia posited a new era in which mechanisation, man, society and nature would supposedly be in harmony. This was his guiding myth, and it is present in his buildings and in his solar symbols on the Capitol. Both Nehru and Le Corbusier grasped that Chandigarh was a national, not just a local project, and both were major figures on the world stage: Nehru as an international statesman, Le Corbusier as a modern architect endowed with a universal vision. As I said at the beginning, I first rolled into Chandigarh on a bus 35 years ago without knowing a soul in India. Since then India, and Chandigarh, have become part of my life. How extraordinary then for me to be standing here on the Capitol celebrating Chandigarh and Le Corbusier 50 years after his death. Such is destiny I suppose. I am also deeply touched that my book *Le Corbusier: Ideas and Forms* is being presented here in this company and in this setting, with the Assembly on one side, and the High Court on the other, for some of my thoughts and insights originated here. The only thing missing at this point is the moon. The sun went down, and I was hoping that a crescent moon might come up to match the planetary curves on the top of the Assembly building.

A CITY BORN IN IDEALISM

Raj Rewal

It's very important to deliberate on the direction the city of Chandigarh should take in the course of the next 25 years, because we are moving very fast and things are changing, what happens now in 5 years used to happen in 25 years. So the next few years are very important with regards what directions we take. I hope the idealism, courage and the wisdom which gave birth to Chandigarh would carry through its journey to the future and that's a very important future for us, because our future for Indian architecture, future for the city and I think to some extent even if I am not exaggerating—future for urbanism, city planning even for international concerns and areas lies in that.

We are going to build more cities in Asia now than ever. We are going to build much more now than we have ever built in the last 100 years in the next 10 years, so I think the direction which we take now is very important because it will pave the way for what can be done. Corbusier was a child of European enlightenment which gave life to rationalism and Modernity. India and Jawaharlal Nehru (India's first prime minister) was looking forward to a future and progress based on scientific temperament. I think it's very important to understand that moment in the history of India, there was a vitality, there was an idealism, there was a thrust for what we are going to do in the future, I was a very young man when all this was happening, in fact, I was partly in Paris at that time and one would hear murmurs in Paris of what Corbusier was achieving with

Facing page:
Chandigarh Framed View
Assembly from High Court
© William J.R. Curtis, 1984

a very young team of Indian architects and planners in Chandigarh. So the confluence and meeting of those two great minds Corbusier and Nehru resulted in Chandigarh.

There was a lot of controversy at the time and there was lot of talk about various aspects of Chandigarh, whether it was too spread out, whether concrete was the right surface for buildings, etc. but I would say that time has shown Chandigarh is now celebrated as one of the greenest cities of not only India, but of the world. I think, for the plantation and the greenery, we have to give credit to the late Dr M.S. Randhawa who took in hand the plantation schemes which were, of course, devised with many other people but he saw them through, so we today have to celebrate the names of some of the people who were there at the beginning. So at this stage we are passing through a critical phase in India where the idealism of Nehru's India is being diluted by consumerist and market economy values; we have to consider that very seriously.

Imagine an engineer and an administrator from Punjab—P.L. Varma and P.N. Thapar respectively—who went to Europe looking for the world's finest architect and town planner around 1949-1950, chose Corbusier on the spot to come to India and design the city. It has to be said, though Corbusier was well known at the time as a visionary, as an artist though he had not built so extensively. I think Chandigarh gave him an ideal palette, a virgin land where he could explore ideas to his great abilities. A tribute is due to Varma and Thapar; constituting the search team, for finding the right person for the job.

I hope we have some people listening now that how this thing was done at the time, and why can't we replicate it now? Because if we are going to go ahead that should be remembered very well. Today, I have to say that the way these team members driven by the idealism with which they went, and chose one single person by themselves—if it was to be done today, they may well be hauled up by the Central Vigilance Commission because this was not done through the tender process!

I think this must be remembered now because I this idealism of choosing the best is now giving way to the lowest tender process because there is some consumerist attitude, etc. This should be thrown in the dustbin in my opinion, if we want to carry out quality work, not only in Chandigarh but also in the rest of India. I also take this opportunity to mention the enormous contribution made by the highly motivated, energetic Indian architects and town planners working along with the Corbusean team that made Chandigarh possible and, what it is today.

Somebody mentioned to me in France that Corbusier was an artist, a visionary, but it's actually the approach and the diligence of the Indian town planners which made Chandigarh what it is, so I think they have to be remembered very much too. So there is a generation which has passed away, but there is still a generation that can contribute here. I would like to really thank the organisers for the symposium because I had come here about six months ago and seen the dismal situation of all these areas; I had seen junkies sitting in the great promenade, under the Tower of Shadows next to the various buildings.

I think the present administration has done an enormous work to clean up all that mess. But I hope they carry it through and it's not as a one time occasion, that is done for an event, it should be for all time. The Capitol Complex should be open to the citizens for easy access and not taken over by the security people. Because then it presents a dismal situation when you come, you see barbed wire only, you see all sorts of things which I'm not going to mention now.

So I would really like to thank the organisers of the symposium who made it possible for all of us to come here and to contribute.

INTRODUCTION

Le Corbusier and Chandigarh merit constant re-visitations

Rajnish Wattas
Deepika Gandhi

A genius like Le Corbusier, unequivocally acclaimed as 20th century's greatest architect, urban planner, theorist, painter and much more, is such a rich and deep reservoir of ideas, forms, innovations and transformations that despite numerous existing publications, yet more can be mined.

As historians look back at his epic repertoire of work; if one single place epitomises his entire lifetime's range of creativity more than any other, it is Chandigarh. Quite naturally, ongoing periodic reflections and discourses on the subject are happening and need to continue. For, Chandigarh was conceived not just as a model city for India but a laboratory of architecture and urban planning for the entire world. And there are no full stops to this churning.

Though, he developed numerous hypothetical urban theories for the city of future and urban renewal projects such as that for Paris and other cities in the world, none ever got realised. By the time he arrived in Chandigarh well past 60 years of age, he was in his creative prime and his ideas and work was being received with great significance and worldwide publicity. Surely, an icon by then he was initially reluctant to take up the Chandigarh project, but perhaps some 'cosmic connect' between the Indian team comprising P.L. Varma the Chief Engineer and P.N. Thapar the Chief Administrator for the 'Punjab New Capital Project' convinced him of the provincial government's sincerity in building what he would create. The rest is history.

The idea of building a new capital city was conceived by the Punjab Government after India's partition in 1947 and the resultant loss of its erstwhile capital city of Lahore, with its going to the Pakistan side. After the initial work done by the American team that had to abruptly abort with the tragic loss of its key member Mathew Nowicki, the Punjab Government engaged Le Corbusier in 1951 as a replacement.

After more than six and a half decades of phenomenal growth, Chandigarh planned for merely half a million people is today nearly 1.2 million and still growing. Quite ironically, the city by offering excellent quality of life along with very good work, education and healthcare facilities has become a victim of its phenomenal success. It now faces humungous challenges of coping up with unbridled growth straining it's already over stretched infrastructure, services, greenery—yet preserving its unique architectural character and heritage.

The crowning glory for Chandigarh's success story was stamped on 16 July 2016 when its Capitol Complex designed by Le Corbusier was inscribed by UNESCO in its World Modern Heritage List as part of a trans-serial nomination of 17 of his works worldwide. Even before this, two historic events recognising Capitol Complex as an outstanding architectural ensemble took place earlier. First, when the Indian Prime Minister, Narendra Modi, chose it as the venue to receive the then French President Francois Hollande on his visit to the country on 24 January 2016 and later on 21 June same year, when a mega event in which 30,000 people participated jointly to celebrate the World Yoga Day, led by the Prime Minister Modi himself. Surely he sensed the power and beauty of its architectural settings, vibrant enough to choose it amongst many other options available for such landmark occasions.

THE CHANDIGARH SYMPOSIUM

In October 2015, the Chandigarh Administration organised a major international symposium 'Celebrating Le Corbusier's Chandigarh: 50 years after the master' in which eminent architects, urban planners, historians and critics participated from all over the world and India. The three-day event attended by more than 800 delegates was a huge success and spawned many new ideas and issues for further discourse. The inaugural event was befittingly held at the main plaza of Corbusier's Capitol Complex amidst the twilight splendour of the illuminated edifices of the Assembly, High Court, Secretariat and the various other monuments. This atmosphere enabled moments of historic visualisation of the sculptural and enigmatic forms created by the master architect, seen in new light. A full scale mock-up of the unbuilt Governor's Palace too was specially erected for the event.

William Curtis in his keynote address quite succinctly put the stature of both Le Corbusier and Chandigarh in perspective, 'It is a city of national foundation and of personal re-foundation'. And on the oft-debated question 'Is Chandigarh an Indian city?' his words, 'India is a place that rethinks its own architectural history, every so often, even on a grand scale. Fatehpur Sikri, for example, absorbed and transformed ideas from diverse earlier traditions in a new synthesis mirroring Akbar's inclusive model of imperial rule. In a sense, the Capitol in Chandigarh does this too but with a democratic and inclusive imperative for a post-colonial, secular nation state'.

Chandigarh was not only the venue but also thematically the fulcrum around which all intellectual churnings of the symposium took place. The city epitomises Corbusier's *tour de force* and culmination of his lifetime's work where he got full opportunity to test and implement all his architectural theories and ideas to usher in Modernism in the world. It was his tryst with destiny.

The issues and reflections generated through presentations made by the various participants, panel discussions and audience interactions led to a very valuable corpus of fresh understandings of Corbusier's fathomless depth of genius. Such a rich material surely merited documentation, further comment and discourse. And thus was born the idea of the book *Le Corbusier Rediscovered: Chandigarh and beyond.*

It was prudent that such a book doesn't become another standard 'proceedings of conference' kind of publication. Therefore, well after the event, all the contributors were requested to pen down their essays afresh, while sticking broadly to the themes presented by them at the symposium—yet free to update, expand and modify them suitably enough to collectively form one cogent, meaningful document.

Though, the process for the Capitol Complex to be inscribed in the UNESCO World Heritage list was very much on at the time of the Symposium, the official approval came nearly a year later. This honour not only heightens fresh worldwide focus on the Capitol Complex alone, but also puts the spotlight on the whole of Chandigarh city and its creator Le Corbusier.

SCOPE AND STRUCTURE OF THE BOOK

While this book celebrates, explores and revisits many of Corbusier's ideas—this is not done in isolation but in the context of time, space and with the perspective of the users of his buildings as well as the citizens of the city. With the dimension of time, the green fields of the Chandigarh site that Corbusier worked upon is totally a different place now. It is above all else a living heritage. Both Chandigarh and other Indian cities are undergoing a humongous, vibrant growth. A buoyant economy, aspirational new generation and the government's focus on revitalising urban areas pose myriad challenges for the Indian architects and planners.

Chandigarh's Capitol Complex is still an incomplete composition with the Governor's Palace unbuilt, as are some other smaller connecting elements and landscape features. It was felt that the decision on undertaking such a task belatedly has to be well considered bearing in mind the challenge of maintaining authenticity of the original design. The mixed response to the completion of Corbusier's Saint-Pierre church at Firminy, France, completed in 2006, 41 years after his death is a case in point.

Numerous other issues were discussed, such as how relevant it is to try and conserve all Corbusean structures in Chandigarh, and how to decide the relative value of their architectural heritage? How to find the right balance between the officially declared heritage component of the city and the rest of it where burgeoning populations are stressing services and infrastructure resulting in clamour for more need-based changes? Growth of cities in the developing world demands different strategies than those adopted in developed countries. Chandigarh still inspires a renewed utopian search for the 21st century's ideal city, not only for India but for the entire developing world.

Therefore the book with its diverse, yet, thematically linked sections and the seamlessly blended together essays covered by them, hopes to become a significant entity in its own right; beyond the intellectual scope of the Symposium.

KEY ISSUES

The book has been organised in various sections that build up the overall theme of the book in a sequential and interconnected narrative. The seemingly independent and 'disparate' essays while complete in themselves, are all actually links to a collective whole and the separate dots get connected finally in the book as one entity.

Section One of the book on the theme 'Le Corbusier: The timeless in Modern' comprises of the essay 'Le Corbusier's Capitol in Chandigarh as a Cosmic and Political Landscape' by Wiliam J.R. Curtis. It decodes the myriad enigmas of Corbusier's architecture, 'His individual works are like dense poetic texts combining many levels of meaning over a hermetic core. Just when the historian imagines that an "explanation" has been found, the buildings slip away from the grasp of rationalisation, re-asserting their right to live in the realm of space, form, material and experience.'

Complimenting this exploration of Corbusier's genius, B.V. Doshi—the only Indian architect who worked with the master on Chandigarh's Capitol Complex project in his Paris office and later on his works in Ahmedabad close hand—provides rare, first-hand insights into the way Corbusier 'played the game' of inventing and reinventing his 'tool kit' of architecture. In the essay 'The Indian Incarnation' he shares, 'Why and how he designed the buildings the way he did...what he was before in Paris and what he was still in Paris, he was not the same in India, particularly in case of architecture in Chandigarh and Ahmedabad.' He adds that, 'Architecture was a serious game for him but it's a game of learning, acquiring, enjoying and experiencing.'

In 'Le Corbusier and the question of Brutalism' Jacques Sbriglio fascinatingly opens up new windows of appreciation of the deeper aesthetic beauty lying beneath Corbusier's seemingly 'rough expression' of concrete buildings. He writes, 'They attempt to mix construction technologies ranging from the most archaic to the most sophisticated, to finally

Facing page and above:
The symposium 'Celebrating
Le Corbusier's Chandigarh'
in session
Source: Chandigarh College
of Architecture, Chandigarh

establish astonishing relationships between all disciplines of the arts, what Le Corbusier called *la synthèse des arts,* or the artistic symbiosis.'

Then the book in a very natural flow moves onto to Section Two titled: 'Le Corbusier's imprint: India and Beyond' comprising essays 'Le Corbusier Redirected: A brief history of his influence in Venezuela' by Alfredo Brillembourg and 'Le Corbusier: Impacting post-Independence architecture' by Raj Rewal. These two essays reflect the huge geographical sweep of Corbusier's influence ranging from Venezuela to India, inspiring and educating the next generations of architects as a catalyst of Modernism in those worlds.

Brillembourg writes about Corbusier's pioneering influence in bringing Modernism to emerging nations and coexistence of formal as well as informal urbanism. 'His Domino House, designed in 1914 as a housing prototype meant to respond to a wartime Europe, epitomizes flexibility, the open plan, and early modern housing as a whole....Concrete slabs provide not only a versatile platform for different interior layouts and needs, but also a foundation for further upward growth. Corbusier lives on not only in the Modernist towers of Caracas, but in the concrete and brick slums surrounding them as well.' This is perhaps fairly true of most of the emerging countries world over.

After the work of Corbusier in India a new generation of foreign-trained Indian architects began searching for creating a national identity amidst the universal language of Modernism.

As Raj Rewal notes, 'Corbusier's ability to transcend his own considerable design vocabulary to explore an architectural expression for each building.... It was the expressive force of Corbusier's architecture that hit me. The metaphors and symbols can be read differently in Corbusier's works but the important lesson for me was that architecture can express diverse feelings; it can be executed in the new language of our time and Modernism need not be sterile.'

With the conferment of the UNESCO Heritage status to the Capitol Complex, Section Three of the book, 'Chandigarh's Heritage is world Heritage' becomes even more critical. The essay by S.D. Sharma on 'Le Corbusier's Capitol: Completing the incomplete' brings fresh perspective to the long-pending issue of building the crucial unbuilt fourth edifice of the Capitol ensemble that is the Governor's Palace/Museum of Knowledge and the connecting landscape elements (though only sketchy concepts exist). Now, nearly six decades after it was designed, many architects and scholars feel that it should be built, but, with an adapted reuse of the same design. On the other hand, some critics of the proposal consider it a 'risky adventure' compromising on Corbusier's authenticity of concept and detail. Hopefully a broad consensus emerges and the sad, gaping void that still stares one in this great Complex is filled up to become finally a 'finished symphony'.

Fortunately for the world Le Corbusier was aware of his place in history and with great foresight in his own lifetime set up a custodian of all his works: architectural drawings, sketches, paintings, sculptures and documents, etc. 'Archiving, exhibiting and disseminating Le Corbusier's legacy: A Foundation and a Modern Art Collection' by Michel Richard, Director of the Fondation Le Corbusier, Paris, elaborates on the huge role played by the Foundation in the preservation of all his legacy systematically, and efficiently making it available for all scholars and researchers for continued reference and interpretations. Besides all this, it also undertakes numerous other activities like organizing expositions and publishing literature on Corbusier from time to time.

This section is rounded off with, 'Chandigarh: City in Garden—Trees as elements of urban design' by Rajnish Wattas where a lesser publicised aspect of the city: its meticulously planned landscaping with special focus on trees is highlighted. As one of the very few or perhaps the only city of such a size with planned landscaping, Chandigarh is today considered the most liveable and humane city of the country. It holds pride of place in having the highest tree canopy cover in India and the lowest air pollution. This makes it a model, green, urban habitat with lessons for other cities world over.

The main thematic essays by the global participants close down in Section Four titled, 'Chandigarh: Garden City to Smart City'. This takes the narrative of the book beyond the immediacy of Corbusier and Chandigarh to the larger issues of urbanisation in India and a search for the ideal Indian City; including a makeover of Chandigarh for its unbridled future growth. A city is always an evolving, living and growing organism. 'The

Chandigarh Master Plan 2031: A vision for the future of the 'City Beautiful' by Sumit Kaur elaborates on the future template for Chandigarh's growth in the next 15-20 years. Besides the original Corbusean layout plan of the city no master plan with statutory legal backing existed till this document was prepared to ensure the City's orderly future growth protecting its ethos and heritage on one hand and on the other, meeting future demands generated by growth and altered geo-political settings.

A glimpse of the future road to be taken by Chandigarh is revealed in 'Avant Le Smart Le Corbusier: Reinventing Chandigarh in the age of Smart Cities' by Jagan Shah. It illustrates how Chandigarh the visionary city of India is so well positioned for evolving into a 'Smart City'—a huge scheme undertaken by the Indian Government for revitalisation and renewal of cities across the country and optimizing their sustainability while bringing forth the best civic services. 'Indeed, the replicable planning of the Smart City proposal for Chandigarh can result in a complete rejuvenation of the city', opines Shah. Over the period, 'the city's economic driver has been changed from an administrative and residential centre to a centre for tourism, it now needs to service and entertain and do business with a larger floating population of tourists, increasing footfalls in public spaces that have been largely devoid of people.'

In a counter viewpoint to Jagan Shah's assertion Rahul Mehrotra in 'Urban India: Towards a Smart Urban Turn' presents an alternate vision than one held popularly in the establishment. He urges emphatically to be watchful against populist forces driven by 'hungry capital' turning cities into gentrified elitist islands of the haves with little affordable room for the under-privileged. 'The increasing concentration of global flows in urban centres has exacerbated the inequalities and spatial divisions between social classes...Smart Cities should make planning lead the way become *Avant garde* once again and not be obsessed just with capital and technology but instead equally emphasize that cities should aspire to be humane centric in their conceptualization and formulation,' he adds.

To make the book a journey down the memory lane in Section Four 'From the Archives' some rare memoirs by two key Indian teammates of Le Corbusier who shouldered the pioneering work done by the then dedicated team have been included. 'Corbusier's Brave New World: Personal Impressions' by P.L. Varma and 'Le Corbusier as I knew Him' by M.N. Sharma have been added. While Varma was the Chief Engineer of the Chandigarh project and one of the two-member team sent by the Punjab Government to visit Europe to select a suitable architect for its new capital; Sharma was the first Indian architect to be recruited for the team. He was not only witness to Corbusier and his working first hand; but also one of the few who had worked with the Mayer team also, that preceded Corbusier's arrival. Memoirs of such key persons give a ringside view of the vintage Chandigarh and its pioneering days.

The last Section 'Endnotes' presents a collage of the year-long events that were a build-up to the October 2015 Symposium. To update the book to the present the write-up 'Capitol Complex: Road to UNESCO leads ahead' elaborates on the massive preparations and spade work done by the Chandigarh Administration, leading the City to finally earn the much-coveted UNESCO Heritage tag. Photo-essays and montages of rarely before seen archival moments and contemporary views of the city and the spruced up Capitol Complex, have been especially added to visually enrich the book.

SUMMING UP...

Even in its present incomplete state Chandigarh's Capitol Complex has acquired the UNESCO World Heritage status, thereby imparting a reflected glory to the entire city in fact. The challenge now is to safeguard it for posterity. 'Through his extraordinary process of invention and transformation, Le Corbusier created something reaching well beyond the scope of his own references and his own time. Dense in meaning, powerful in its forms, it aspires towards universality' aptly says William Curtis.

Chandigarh has been called, 'a city born in idealism'. Hopefully, this book will help in keeping that spirit alive.

LE CORBUSIER

THE TIMELESS IN MODERN

LE CORBUSIER'S CAPITOL IN CHANDIGARH AS A COSMIC AND POLITICAL LANDSCAPE

William J.R. Curtis

There are no shortcuts when coming to terms with the architecture of Le Corbusier. His individual works are like dense poetic texts combining many levels of meaning over a hermetic core. Just when the historian imagines that an 'explanation' has been found, the buildings slip away from the grasp of rationalisation, re-asserting their right to live in the realm of space, form, material and experience. Le Corbusier's architecture seems to possess an infinite capacity to stir both enthusiasm and animosity. As his contribution recedes further into history, new readings and transformations become possible. Le Corbusier's prototypes, built and unbuilt, continue to stimulate invention. His vast creative universe is apparently capable of inspiring later architects of contrasting creeds and forms, perhaps because Le Corbusier himself delighted in polarities. He continues to function as both a mirror and a lens, helping individuals to define their own artistic identity and to focus upon generic problems. Rather as Picasso did for painting and sculpture, Le Corbusier redefined some of the ground rules of the architectural discipline.

Works of architecture of any depth inhabit time on several levels and at variable wave-lengths. There is first of all the short-wave of actuality, of the present: buildings may crystallise a contemporary situation with all of its contradictions and confusions. But they also grow out of earlier experiences and out of an unfolding tradition combining personal and period strands. The deeper and more penetrating the individual invention

Facing page:
View past Assembly towards
High Court, Chandigarh
© William J.R. Curtis, 2014

P. xlviii:
Bas relief of modular man at
Assembly building, Chandigarh
Photo courtesy: Chandigarh
Administration

the harder it is to fit it into any chronological or stylistic slot. Works of real power and resonance cut back further in time, sometimes transforming ancient ideas and time-worn principles, but in a radically altered form. Beyond these long-wave motions in history there are possibly even further layers before one comes to a sort of bedrock, a substratum of features which are fundamental to the medium of architecture itself, and which may even engage with visible or invisible features of the natural world.

Le Corbusier constantly absorbed new experiences and perceptions (for example in his travel sketches), then stocked these in his memory where they underwent a 'sea-change' (to borrow a phrase from Shakespeare's Tempest), before being translated into the stuff of his own dreams, myths and inventions. He stole things from the world because they corresponded to some inner patterns of thought and imagination. In this process, abstraction played a role in filtering experience and in translating particular things into generalised icons and emblems. Painting served him as a laboratory. Le Corbusier was a sort of magician who would take things from their original context and transform them into his own terms. Thus an ocean liner could turn into a housing scheme, a crab's shell into a chapel roof, a freeway into an 'S' shaped ramp. Le Corbusier's creative intelligence discerned unexpected analogies or 'correspondences' between diverse phenomena, so that an open hand might resemble both a tree and a flying dove, or the curves of a woman might coalesce into the sinuous outline of a landscape, then to emerge as an abstract calligraphy with no particular association.

This preamble on architectural invention may be useful in coming to terms with the genesis of the Capitol in Chandigarh which occupied Le Corbusier for the last 15 years of his life between 1951 and 1965. Chandigarh was one of the 'Foundation documents' of the newly independent Indian Republic and as such was automatically implicated in societal projections and nationalist myths in a period of post-colonial re-definition. For Le Corbusier this was the chance at last to plan an entire city according to principles which had been maturing over a lifetime, although in fact, once he had set the ground rules in place he left most of the realisation of the city to others such as Pierre Jeanneret, Maxwell Fry, Jane Drew and the Indian architects who flocked to join the experiment. Instead he concentrated almost exclusively upon the monumental ensemble of the Capitol to the north eastern extremity of

Facing page:
Le Corbusier, Master Plan for Phase 1 of Chandigarh
© FLC-ADAGP

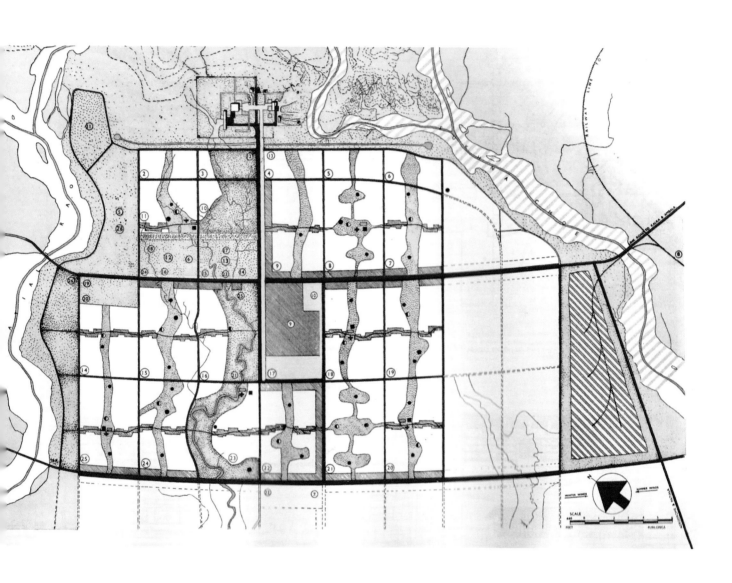

the city which was deliberately defined as a separate zone by means of earthworks and mounds. The general layout of the new city relied to some degree upon a pre-existing plan by the American architect Albert Mayer but also fused together features of Le Corbuier's *Ville Radieuse*, British cantonments, Lutyens' New Delhi, Parisian axes and vistas, in fact a range of sources which had been part of Le Corbusier's mental furniture for some time.

Le Corbusier's major urban proposals of the 1920s such as the *Ville Contemporaine* (1922) achieved a monumental scale through the use of grand axes, vast spaces, hierarchies of parks, formal geometry and carefully composed arrays of skyscrapers but they did not pay much attention to questions of civic representation. However, with his proposals for competitions such as those for the League of Nations in Geneva (1927) and for the Palace of the Soviets in Moscow (1931), the architect began to define a language of modern monumentality drawing together interior and exterior spaces of assembly. With the proposal for the Mundaneum (1929), to stand above Lac Léman, Le Corbusier integrated grand gestures such as a stepped pyramid, formally grouped skyscrapers and processional routes for cars and pedestrians, with controlled views of the surrounding landscape, including the mountains in the distance. In these cases, his utopian vision seemed to imply the harmonisation of the machine age with 'Nature'. As one follows Le Corbusier's trajectory through the 1930s and the 1940s one becomes aware of his interest in the symphonic scale of landscape and territory (for example in his travel sketches or in his diverse proposals for Algiers and Rio de Janeiro). In turn there seems to be an ever increasing engagement with the idea of public places as major elements of urban design, for example in the proposal for the reconstruction of the centre of St Dié (1946) which implied a latter day idea of a *forum*. Le Corbusier's sensibility was ever more attentive to the role of landscape and of surrounding topography in urbanism.

The Capitol in Chandigarh combines buildings and open spaces in an artificial landscape. It is an incomplete project. The Parliament, High Court and Secretariat were constructed but not the Governor's Palace at the top of the ensemble. The landscaping is also not finished. Le Corbusier envisaged a sculpted terrain incorporating monumental buildings, platforms, bodies of water, terraces, trees, parks, roads, valleys

Facing page above:
Capitol Complex, Chandigarh, seen from roof of Secretariat
© William J.R. Curtis, 1988

Facing page below:
Le Corbusier, overall site plan of Capitol with elevations of Secretariat, Assembly, Governor's Palace and High Court. Scale 1/1000. Drawn in LeC Atelier by Talati 8/02/1956
© FLC-ADAGP

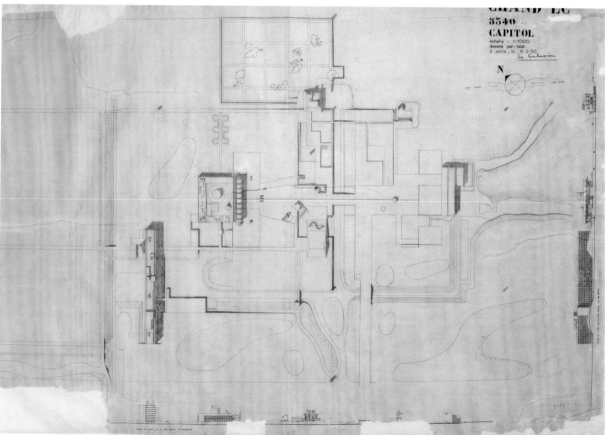

and gardens alluding to several past styles. For example, next to the Governor's Palace he suggested a gridded garden based upon Mogul examples; elsewhere he thought of using looping roads as in Central Park, New York. This symphonic ensemble of the natural and the artificial combines some recognizable images with signs and symbols of a more emblematic character. The buildings themselves are not separable from this dense 'text', as they reiterate guiding themes but in a more abstract form. Part of the interest of the Capitol resides in Le Corbusier's combination of democratic monumentality with a recognisable public art of representation. He hoped to create an entirely new sort of urban space with a certain mythic presence heightening the experience of the surroundings, for example the foothills of the Himalayas in the distance, but also suggesting the visible and invisible forces of 'Nature' as a spiritualised concept and haunting presence. Le Corbusier took over the 'progressive' aspects of the social programme and injected them with his own utopian mythology concerning a supposed harmony between human beings, their institutions, and what he thought of as the "laws" of the natural world. One may think of the Capitol in Chandigarh as a 'cosmic and political landscape'.

To understand Le Corbusier's interpretation of Indian realities, both recent and more distant, it is necessary to consider the very *raison d'être* of the new city. Chandigarh was created out of the hopes, chaos and tragedy surrounding the Independence of India in 1947, and the subsequent Partition in 1948 which led to the creation of Pakistan. The state of the Punjab was cut in two and the old capital of Lahore was left on the Pakistani side. Needed then was a city to house innumerable refugees but also to supply an administrative head to the Indian Punjab and to anchor and stabilise a crucial part of northern Indian territory. This emergency situation was translated into a major opportunity when Nehru understood that the new city could in turn become a show-piece of the newly independent nation. It could reflect his cherished ideals of balanced technological modernisation (with the socialist state playing a major role in guiding the economy); democratic representational government (with parliament, senate, justice, governor independent but in equilibrium); and secularism (with a framework of citizenship and social rights independent of questions of religion or caste). Although it was to be a mere local state capital, Chandigarh could take on national even international significance.

When Chandigarh was in construction Nehru referred to it as a 'temple of the new India...unfettered by tradition.' The entire mood of those times was to construct a better future and to forget years of colonial occupation which had often forced Indians to live in extremely cramped and unhygienic conditions in the old cities. The themes of open space, greenery and light which were so dear to Le Corbusier, touched many chords with members of an elite whose values were to some degree 'western'. Political independence for India permitted the planning of a national future but also a reassessment of the past. 'She [India] is waking up....intact at a time when all is possible', wrote Le Corbusier to Nehru: 'But India is hardly a brand new country: it has lived through the highest and most ancient civilizations. It has an intelligence, moral philosophy and conscience of its own.' India also happened to possess one of the greatest architectural heritages in world history, and of this too Le Corbusier was fully aware. This was another side of his task: to acknowledge India's spiritual and artistic traditions but without lapsing into superficial imitation or orientalism. It was a question of probing

Indian culture to its roots, its deeper patterns of myth and meaning, then transforming these substructures into modern symbolic forms. The problem was not so foreign to an architect who had always linked authentic modernity to the radical reappraisal of the past.

When Le Corbusier first came to India in 1951 he was quick to grasp these larger political agendas. He was also inspired by, even overwhelmed by, the selected site, a drainage plain containing several villages but with extraordinary views in the direction of the foothills of the Himalayas. He realized that brick and reinforced concrete would be his most likely materials, especially given the abundance of clay and the indigenous expertise in concrete construction on the part of Indian engineers. He responded to the climate with its extreme heat and rains as a stimulus in finding an appropriate vocabulary. In his Indian sketchbooks he referred to deep loggias, verandas, shading devices, cross ventilation, plants and water. The smaller commissions in Ahmedabad (Sarabhai House, Millowner's Association Building, Shodhan House etc.) were like laboratories. He soon established the basic 'key' or 'genotype' for his Indian works: the *parasol'*, an overhanging, protective roof held up on slender supports, providing shelter from the sun and the rain, but also providing cross ventilation underneath through sun shading blades or *brise-soleil* (sunbreakers). In effect the *parasol* was a transformation of the topmost slab of the *Dom-Ino* skeleton although there was the intervening discovery of the shading roof of the Maison Baizeau in Tunis of 1928. Variations on the *'parasol* theme' can be found in all of the main buildings on the Capitol in Chandigarh.

The Capitol is the symbolic 'head' of Chandigarh, a city which suggests an abstraction of the body with the 'spine' of the main axial road and the 'arms' of the main transversal one. The Capitol itself is deliberately removed from the town and constitutes a separate domain. In defining this area Le Corbusier had to balance many considerations. He needed to define limits yet make the most of the epic views. He reverted to a fundamental device for establishing a collective space, the platform, although he also worked downwards to define trenches for traffic and upwards to establish the levels and terraces of the actual buildings. In plan he worked with axes and cross axes but these were rarely directly aimed at buildings in an obvious way, they were usually 'slipped' and displaced to create a dynamic tension. The Capitol is a subtle overlay of geometries and grids combining several symmetries and asymmetries at diverse scales. It splices together devices of classical planning such as processional routes and hierarchy, with rotational spatial ideas that seem to stem from modern abstract painting (e.g. Mondrian), with others again which may derive from the plans of Mogul and Pre-Mogul palace complexes and gardens. In the Capitol there is tension between the orthogonal geometry of the main buildings, which follows that of the city grid, and the diagonal geometry following the path of the sun at the equinox, which is dramatised in, for example, the roof scape of the Assembly building. With the help of masts Le Corbusier established the main distances while regulating these with the harmonics of his system the Modulor.

What Le Corbusier later referred to as a 'battle of spaces in the mind' took into account the direct experience of the landscape but also the meaning of the institutions. On the Capitol the buildings are sensed in an ever-changing dialogue of spatial relationships and framed views. Le Corbusier set them far apart so that justice could be independent of the parliament and the executive (and vice-versa) in a graphic demonstration of the balance of powers. His spatial conception of a shared landscape also had to do with openness, the opposite of tyranny. He established some of the terms of a 'democratic monumentality' expressing the strength of institutions of state, but avoiding authoritarian oppressiveness. The buildings are rarely perceived as frontal forms and seen on the diagonal deflect the eye in a perspective towards the surroundings. The naked concrete forms dramatized by light and gashed by shade have an ancient feeling and yet these masses seem to float in space. They combine a brute directness with a refined, linear sense in their profiles.

The oblong form of the Secretariat is deliberately subsidiary in the composition, as it contains the bureaucracy for carrying out the decisions made on the basis of the representational process. Missing is the crowning element of the ensemble, the Governor's Palace with its surrounding waterways, valleys, ramps and formal gardens. Without these elements, the Capitol 'leaks' towards the north-east and loses some of its tension and scale. It also loses something of its meaning, for all of Le Corbusier's buildings in his total project for the Capitol were variations upon the same basic themes, as in a symphonic structure in music. Nehru cancelled the Governor's Palace because he feared that it would be 'undemocratic', but the proposal is known from sketches, drawings and models, moreover there are no precise drawings for the crucial landscaping of valleys and pools which are integral to the project. Le Corbusier's basic idea was a compact building with several horizontal layers traversed by an ascending *promenade architecturale* which would have emerged on the roof under a *parasol* in the form of an upturned crescent. In effect this was like an abstraction of the gesturing 'Open Hand' nearby, but it was also a symbolic form capable of several functions and meanings. There are echoes of bull's horns, of planetary paths, of an outdoor theatre, even of the idea of an *impluvium* for gathering rain. If an imperial dome suggests a downward force, this crescent suggests liberation towards space and sky.

Like all the buildings on the Capitol, the Governor's Palace was designed to be seen frontally, from the sides, or on the diagonal. A sketch of 1952 showing the water gardens and levels recalls the Diwan-i-Khas (or Private Audience Hall) at Fatehpur Sikri, the complex designed for the

Mogul emperor Akbar in the late 16th century. The cosmic world axis and a roof open to solar forces also finds a possible echo in Le Corbusier's project for the Governor's Palace. The '*chattri*' or dome on piers (like an umbrella) is found in both Mogul and Rajput examples. Perhaps Le Corbusier's crescent shape on piers is a transformation of this inherited element. It should not be forgotten that in its time the Palace and Mosque complex of Fatehpur Sikri was a capitol of sorts embodying Akbar's political ambition of including all creeds and cultures in a new ideal state. A foundation document in its time, it also absorbed and transformed past architectures in a new supposedly universalising symbolism. Moreover its objects and spaces, platforms and levels, shifting axes and compressed vistas articulated the institutions of state in a sort of cosmic theatre. In turn the architecture was realised on the basis of a standardised grammar of trabeation, a *Dom-Ino* skeleton system of a kind, *avant la lettre*, but made from resilient sandstone rather than reinforced concrete.

Le Corbusier's drawings for the Governor's Palace show a foreground of sunken levels with reflecting water pools, ramps, a column and a tree on an island. It was very important, given the secular intentions of the Indian political order, not to appeal to the imagery or traditions of any particular religion or community (Hindu, Moslem, Sikh, Jain etc.), yet Le Corbusier seems to have felt all the same that there was a place for a numinous or spiritual presence in his landscape statement. His abstract

Facing page:
Model of Capitol Complex:
a symbolic landscape
© FLC-ADAGP

Below left:
Diwan-i-Khas, Fatehpur
Sikri, late 16th C AD
© William J.R. Curtis, 1983

Below right:
Le Corbusier, sketch of
project for Governor's
Palace, Chandigarh, April
1952. Album Nivola
© FLC-ADAGP

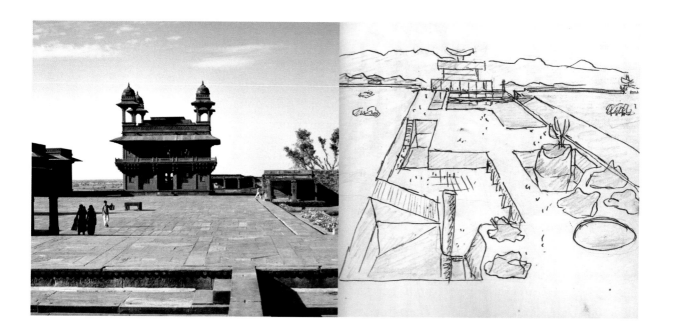

forms are powerful in and of themselves but they also seem to compress together many things, at times hinting at well known symbols such as the column of Ashoka (the first Buddhist Emperor of India who instituted the '*dhama*' or sense of rule), the solar wheel of the law (another Buddhist symbol, appropriated by the modern nation state of India in its flag), or the shape of horns (which could in some circumstances suggest a Shivaite association). But the very abstraction of the forms disallows a collapse into a single reading and so avoids overt identification with any particular community or past historical period. In effect, Le Corbusier may here have embodied a nationalist aspiration of absorbing all parties into a single state with a new official history. More than that, there may have been an international message here. Le Corbusier's modernity consists, precisely, in his capacity to reorder the lexicon, to give old words new meanings, and to 'universalise' the specific, in this case around his utopian agenda of a modern social order in harmony with the forces of 'Nature'. This was Le Corbusier's own version of 'Nature', to be sure, and here it was sacralised.

The High Court is an open hall of justice, a clear expression of availability and rule, a parasol turned into a huge portico with an overhanging roof which also functions as a sluice to siphon off the monsoons into water basins by means of spouts. The individual courtrooms are inserted underneath as a secondary system. P.L.Varma, the main 'client' ('the soul of Chandigarh') was told by Le Corbusier that the basic idea of this structure was 'the strength, the majesty and the shelter of the Law'. It is typical of Le Corbusier's power of metamorphosis that he could think simultaneously of diverse inspirations: modern engineering feats such as dams and sluices; the section of airplane wings; ancient Roman ruins like the Basilica of Maxentius/Constantine in the Roman Forum (which Le Corbusier had sketched and photographed as a young man); even possibly another Mogul type, this time the public audience hall or Diwan-i-Am which sometimes functioned as an open hall of justice, as in the Red Fort in Delhi. The Mogul forts were like encampments of tents frozen in stone and they mapped out the hierarchy and relations of the state. Le Corbusier seems to have captured something of this spirit, but in rigourously modern forms in naked concrete.

The buildings and spaces of the Capitol resemble in some ways Le Corbusier's other late works such as the *Unité d'habitation* in Marseille, the Chapel at Ronchamp and the Monastery of La Tourette. All were

128   VERS UNE ARCHITECTURE

d'une tournure d'esprit : stratégie, législation. L'architecture est sensible à ces intentions, *elle rend*. La lumière caresse les formes pures : *ça rend*. Les volumes simples développent d'immenses surfaces qui s'énoncent avec une variété caractéristique suivant qu'il s'agit de coupoles, de berceaux, de cylindres, de prismes rectangulaires ou de pyramides. Le décor des surfaces (baies) est du même groupe de géométrie. Panthéon, Colisée, aqueducs, pyramide de Cestius, arcs de triomphe, basilique de Constantin, thermes de Caracalla.

Pas de verbiage, ordonnance, idée unique, hardiesse et unité de construction, emploi des prismes élémentaires. Moralité saine.

Conservons, des Romains, la brique et le ciment romain et la pierre de travertin et vendons aux milliardaires le marbre romain. Les Romains n'y connaissaient rien en marbre.

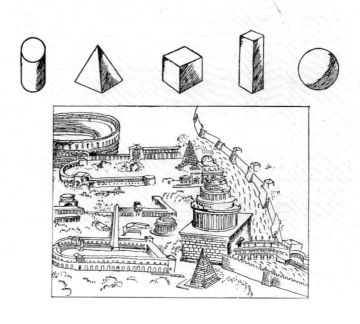

Le Corbusier, sketch of primary solids and ruins of Ancient Rome from *Vers une architecture*, 1923: the presence of the past.
©FLC-ADAGP

realized in rugged materials employing concrete surfaces in a deliberately 'primitivist' manner, and all were concerned with the framing of surrounding landscape as part of an architectural promenade. The robust piers and porticoes of the High Court are surely direct relatives of the massive legs under the *Unité,* while the landscape ensemble of the Capitol is a cousin of that resonance chamber open to the sky, sea and mountains, the roof terrace at Marseille. Quite aside from obvious resemblances of architectural language—bare concrete surfaces, structural piers, curved and inclined walls, light cannons, *brise-soleil, ondulatoires*—the buildings in Chandigarh partake of similar sensibilities to do with complex geometrical intersections, the direct physical presence of architecture, the sense of the body moving through space, the telescoping of landscape views, the use of light and shade to evoke a spiritual dimension. Then there is the matter of gesture, of forms which seem to emit and receive the energy of the setting, of what Le Corbusier sometimes called an *'architecture acoustique'*.

At Chandigarh the curved porticos gesture across space. The tilted scoop of the Assembly combines a sluice for monsoons and a crescent shape while suggesting the action of the hand in an abstract form. Le Corbusier's sketchbooks reveal the extent to which he was looking at humble village structures, carts with huge wheels and crescent shaped chassis, bull's horns and upturned roofs. Beyond Nehru's industrializing agenda, Le Corbusier sensed the importance of Gandhi's vision of the supposed integrity of rural life. The giant revolving door leading into the Assembly

Facing page:
Roman Forum, Basilica of Maxentius / Constantine, 2nd C AD, photo by C.E. Jeanneret (Le Corbusier) taken during his Voyage d'orient, 1911
© FLC-ADAGP

High Court, Chandigarh
© William J.R. Curtis, 1984

is decorated with an enamel painting by Le Corbusier illustrating some of his favourite themes to do with the earthly and celestial realms, a tree of life, animals, the crescent paths of the sun at equinox and solstice, the rhythms of day and night. These parabolic planetary descriptions supply a sort of recognisable code to more abstract versions of similar forms in the roof scape up above.

As one passes into the coolness of the main hall of the building one enters one of the most powerful spaces of assembly in the history of modern architecture. It is the 20th century equivalent to an ancient hypostyle hall with slender concrete mushroom columns rising to a black painted ceiling. This soffit floats in an otherwordly light that creeps in at the edges.

The visitor wanders through this field of columns (which is noble but not overwhelming) and glimpses the huge funnel-like volume of the Assembly chamber which is set off-centre in a way which generates a great dynamism. One reaches this room by means of circumambulation, as if a ritual were intended, as in the movement around a stupa or a place reserved for a cult. As one penetrates, the space explodes upwards towards the sky within the hyperbolic paraboloid volume of the assembly chamber which emerges as a monumental, active form on the

roof scape on top of the building. When one examines the genesis of this arrangement one finds hints in Le Corbusier's notes and sketches. The Assembly building started out as a flat-roofed box but in a sketch of June 1953 the chamber was expressed on the outside as a light tower surrounded by a spiral ramp and the roof was shown as an animated *forum* covered in people. At the bottom of the sheet was another sketch, this time of the cooling towers of a power station near Ahmedabad which had caught Le Corbusier's attention. So many of his ideas involved shifts from one context to another and it may be that he was reflecting upon an appropriate form for lighting and ventilation which might also be suitable to the 'progressive' aspects of the building task.

Le Corbusier also evoked ancient and sacral associations in his design for the Assembly space. A beam of light was to descend into the shadows from the top, on the day of the Opening of the Parliament. In effect this was a microcosm linked to the planetary realm above by means of a solar ray, rather like the Pantheon in Rome, but recalling as well a universal archetype of 'renewal' by means of the energy of light

The High Court in action in the shadows of the giant portico
© William J.R. Curtis, 2014

Facing page above left:
Assembly Building, water basin and village girl, Chandigarh
© William J.R. Curtis, 1985

Facing page above right:
Interior of the Assemby Chamber with acoustic panels as abstracted clouds
© William J.R. Curtis, 2014

Facing page below left:
Le Corbusier, sketch of bulls and peasant houses near Chandigarh, March, 1951.
Album Simla. © FLC-ADAGP

Facing page below right:
Hall of columns in Assembly Building
© William J.R. Curtis, 2014

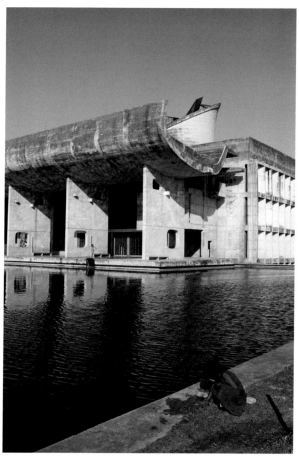

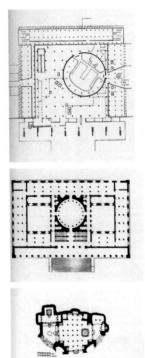

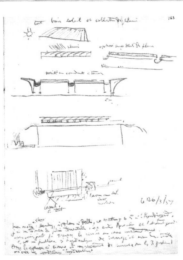

Above:
Assembly Building, Capitol Complex, Chandigarh, view towards ceremonial entrance with enamel door displaying solar symbols and roof scape suggesting cosmic and planetary references. © William J.R. Curtis, 2014

Left:
1. Plan of Assembly Building, Chandigarh
2. Plan of Altes Museum, Berlin, 1827 by Karl F. Schinkel
3. Plan of Elephanta Cave, Mumbai, c 7th C. AD
4. Le Corbusier, sketch proposal for Chandigarh of portico acting as a sluice to evacuate rain of monsoons, 26/03/1951. © FLC-ADAGP

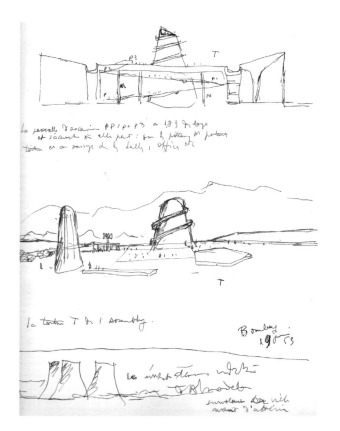

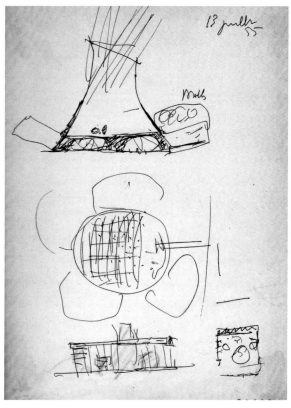

Above
Le Corbusier, sketches of
Assembly comparing roof
lighting system to cooling
towers of power station seen
in Ahmedabad, 1953. Album
Nivola
© FLC-ADAGP

Above right:
Le Corbusier, sketch of
Assembly in plan and section
showing light rays penetrating
'funnel' of Assembly chamber
from above, 13/07/1955
© FLC-ADAGP

Right:
Light penetrating dome of
Pantheon, Rome, 2nd C. AD
© William J.R. Curtis, 1996

(found in ancient Egypt but also in some Hindu temples). Again there was the theme of harmonising human institutions with the 'order' of nature. 'Modern man', he stated with reference to the lighting system of the Parliament, should be reminded that he is a 'son of the sun'. Box, grid, portico, symbolic objects—we could schematise the Parliament in this way, with the tilted pyramid for the senate chamber, and the projecting tower or funnel for the assembly of representatives. The plan has often been compared to that of Schinkel's Altes Museum in Berlin of 1827, although it equally touches upon a basic historical type of portico and dome. The main space inside the Parliament is oriented to the sun's path. On top the tower is capped by a tilted disc with crescent shapes embedded in it—extraordinary sculptural forms with an almost surrealist ambiguity and magic to them, as if they were machine age solar totems. Le Corbusier was inspired by the 18th century Jantar Mantar observatories built by Jai Singh in Delhi and in Jaipur. Reacting to the monumental abstraction of these instruments, he wrote: 'The instruments of Delhi....they point the way: re-link man to the cosmos.... Exact adaptations of forms and organisms to the sun, to the rains, to the air, etc.'

This small fragment of thought stimulated by objects within the Indian tradition is a clue to the entire philosophy behind Le Corbusier's Capitol in Chandigarh. He imagined that India could avoid the worst alienations of industrialism and achieve a new equilibrium between social and natural orders. This pious hope (and illusion!) was expressed in a variety of symbols planned to stand between the main buildings as part of an entire landscape of hillocks, levels, ramps, waterways, and emblematic objects. Among these was an 'S' shape showing the rise and fall of the sun ('the measure of our urban enterprises'), a 'Tower of Shadows' celebrating the mathematics of the Modulor and the various *brise-soleil* (sun-breaker) variations, and an angled ramp leading to a platform suspended between the main buildings. As well as affording a viewing stage this structure, referred to as the 'Martyr's Monument', was to have been animated by a curious figural sculpture of a broken classical column being approached by a tiger (evidently an allegory on the collapse of the British Raj—and not built). Perhaps most important of all, given Le Corbusier's overall intentions in Chandigarh, was the so-called 'Open Hand' hovering on a mast like a gigantic wind vane, although the irreverent observer cannot help thinking of a baseball glove.

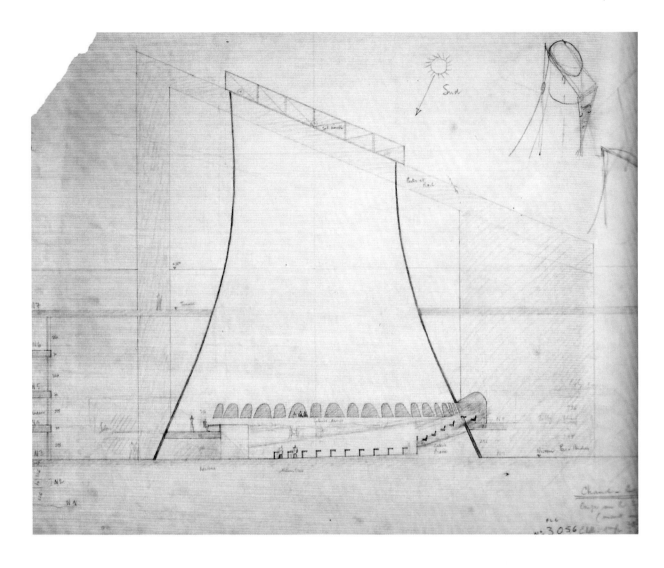

The 'Open Hand' epitomises Le Corbusier's attempt at combining a public iconography with an abstraction permitting several levels of reading and a formal presence permitting multiple relationships to other 'objects' against the sky, such as those on top of the Parliament or the Governor's Palace. As well as a floating hand, Picasso's famous 'Peace Dove' comes to mind. The image also suggests a tree, or an ancient gesture of acceptance and benediction (eg. a Buddhist 'mudra' with the palm of the hand facing outwards and the fingers towards the top). Thus modern popular imagery and ancient imagery to do with acceptance and friendship are combined. Like the bull, the hand was a recurrent theme in Le Corbusier's own paintings. He initially thought of the 'Open Hand' as a symbol of reconciliation above the messy infighting of mundane politics: 'A symbol very appropriate to the new

Section through Assembly Chamber, Drawn in LeC Atelier by Maisonnier 20/09/1953 © FLC-ADAGP

situation of a liberated and independent earth. A gesture which appeals to fraternal collaboration and solidarity between all men and all nations of the earth.'

'Modernity', 'Nature', 'Tradition'—this great triad of Olympian notions is ever present in Le Corbusier's Capitol. His basic materials were space, light, water, reinforced concrete, the sky and the ground. The overall theme was the idealisation of the institutions of the state. The aim was to establish a set of relationships across space between symbolic forms.

The meaning stemmed not only from Le Corbusier's grasp of monumentality, but also from utopian ideas to do with a possible post-colonial world order: the use of technology and man's ingenuity to provide for the needs of all through a proper cultivation and respect for 'Nature'. An idea of this kind is suggested by Le Corbusier's own commentary upon the 'Open Hand' ('open to give, open to receive'), but it also seems to be implied in the solar and natural symbolism of the great enamel door to the Parliament, in the very forms and images of the buildings themselves, and in the vastness of the spatial conception that links the buildings to the distant foothills of the Himalayas. In this manner Le Corbusier hoped to impose a clear order on the chaos of technical modernisation and inevitably he could only fail. Was it not Marx who suggested that a utopia is a hopeless attempt by an individual to change the course of history by imposing a personal project upon it? Le Corbusier referred to himself as an 'acrobat' performing dangerous tricks without being asked to do so: a Don Quixote of a kind

Chandigarh represented a new start for many Indians displaced by the traumas of Partition and it was possibly Le Corbusier's intention that the 'Open Hand' also be understood as a universal image of peace. If so, it is hardly surprising that he should have tried to hitch this image to Nehru's notion of a non-aligned movement in world politics. For Le Corbusier imagined (wrongly given the destructive impact of British imperialism and industry) that India had somehow avoided the ravages of the 'first machine age' of industrialisation and naively hoped that it could now launch off into the 'second machine age', the 'era of harmony', avoiding the extremes of laissez-faire capitalism on the one side, and of communist dictatorship on the other. History did not follow this happy fictional path for the 'third world' of course, and had Le Corbusier returned to earth several years after his death in 1965 he would no doubt have been disturbed by the destructiveness of rapid modernisation and urbanisation. But then perhaps it is the business of monuments to speak about the world as it should be and not as it is? The monuments on the Capitol idealize the institutions of power and reinforce official histories and projections by translating these into the stuff of substantial myth. The cosmological symbols and powerful forms seem to suggest a lost paradise, a landscape of origins, even as they point to an ideal future and evoke an 'eternal present'.

The 'Open Hand' stands out against the horizon, a silhouette which seems held in an arrested movement, like a bird frozen in flight. It hovers above the 'Valley of Contemplation', a rectangular open-air theatre set below ground level, vaguely recalling an ancient Greek state chamber in a ruin. This space is rarely used but in January 1999 it was filled with people for the inauguration of a grand international event, 'Celebrating Chandigarh: 50 Years of the Idea'. Suddenly all the spaces and buildings of the Capitol came alive and were flooded with activity. On this occasion too, a mock-up of the Governor's Palace was constructed from bamboo and cloth like a temporary piece of festival architecture. It served to underline the absence of this key element of the ensemble and the importance of the long distant view to the mountains. For the buildings of the Capitol do not just sit in the landscape, they are an active part of it: they contribute to an overall concept and experience in which the ground has been sculpted into solids and voids affording ever-changing views and juxtapositions. In fact there is a deliberate ambiguity about the ground plane itself, since it is restated on top of the buildings as useable public terraces and open air theatres. What no drawing, literary description or photograph can convey, is the extraordinary telescoping of near and far, the illusions and ambiguities, the way in which the distant hills suddenly become an immediate experience because of a framing device. Without the inheritance of Cubism it is unlikely that Le Corbusier could have achieved these spatial tensions and ambiguities, although it also needs saying that analogous qualities are to be found in the history of Indian architecture.

There is another way of imagining the Capitol and that is from straight above with a full sense of the relief of the terrain, the lines and incisions of the motor traffic valleys, the outlines of the buildings and reflecting

Facing page:
Le Corbusier, Capitol Complex Chandigarh, the Open Hand
© William J.R. Curtis, 2014

surfaces of water. From this vantage point one might grasp the extent to which the whole thing is a pictorial composition or a *bas relief* combining ambiguities of figure and ground, transparencies and illusions of depth, objects, outlines and composed intervals. The meeting of resonant symbolic objects on a plateau and in a framed space recalls Giacometti's Surrealist sculptures of the early 1930s with their primitivist allusions to African games carved into trays of wood. In fact it is the wood models of the Capitol which convey the idea of an artificial landscape most clearly, since they show the extent to which the buildings are embedded between man-made valleys and mounds. Nor should one forget the lake which was created at Varma's insistence and which supplies a welcome area for recreation in the hot months of the year. The way in which the space of the Capitol is compressed and released by the juxtaposition of angles, planes, water surfaces and humps, suggests some of the qualities of 'Land Art' before its time. But it is above all the relationship with the sky which is most astonishing, day and night. The Capitol spaces seem to pull sky forces down to earth and to engage with the sun and the moon. They remind one of Le Corbusier's admiration of another historic Indian city, the 18th century Jaipur, planned according to the precepts of ancient Hindu texts. The astronomical instruments at Jaipur occupy an entire sector of their own in this 'ideal city' and seem to engage actively with the heavens.

There can be little doubt concerning the probity and authenticity of Le Corbusier's monumental buildings on the Capitol, or about the richness of the creative process leading up to them. But the various overt 'signs' and representations raise difficult questions about the social role of public art. Even once the various references to planetary paths, wheels, a hand, etc., have been recognised, to the majority of people it is not clear what these images might mean. They do not, after all, belong to any commonly understood code or realm of shared significance, remaining hermetically sealed in the terminology of Le Corbusier's private universe. Do we have here 'the fiction of a state art, elementary and nonetheless occult, because there is no state religion behind it.'? And as for Le Corbusier's climatic devices they did not always succeed in keeping out the heat and the rain, remaining sometimes rhetorical demonstrations. As for the underlying themes of peace, reconciliation and harmony, these too were in for some rude shocks. In 1966 the State of the Punjab was divided into three to accommodate communal and linguistic differences (a Punjabi

Le Corbusier, Assembly
Building seen across
Capitol, Chandigarh
© William J.R. Curtis, 1984

state and two Hindi ones, Haryana and Himachal Pradesh). At the same time Chandigarh itself became a Union Territory administered from New Delhi. Then in the 1980s the city was besieged by the violence and claims of Sikh separatists. The Capitol was sectored off and divided by checkpoints and fences of barbed wire. The utopian ideal was confronted by base and venial historical reality.

It was suggested earlier that works of architecture may exist in time on several levels and on several wave lengths. They crystallize a situation then history moves on. Surely it is one of the roles of monumental architecture to defy time and to communicate across the ages. Inevitably the original frameworks of iconography slip away—they always do—and just as inevitably new readings are attached at the surface level of signs. But at the deeper level of the vital symbol the work of architecture may go on stirring later generations through the expressive power of its forms, through its continuing presence, gradually to be absorbed into a collective memory. This seems to be the overall situation of the Capitol in Chandigarh. Even in its incomplete state this place has an extraordinary capacity to move people and to touch them at a pre-conscious level. Great architecture communicates before it is understood. Moreover the prototypes of the Capitol beam their messages far and wide. A generation of Indian architects grew up revering Le Corbusier while rejecting his absolutism and his insufficient response to local climate and his lack of sensitivity to both urban and cultural complexity, so his example has been transformed in a critical yet vital way in an Indian branch of Modernism. Le Corbusier's ways of dealing with democratic monumentality and the transformation of lessons from local traditions opened the way for figures as diverse as Kenzo Tange in the Japan of the 1950s and Teodoro Gonzalez de Leon in the Mexico of the 1980s to do something similar in their respective countries.

The visitor who goes to Chandigarh today and wanders onto the Capitol finds an inactive place. The city is still young, is not fully formed, and there continue to be problems of security which inhibit movement and access to the main buildings and spaces. It would be unwise in the present 'free market' atmosphere in India to give way to developer pressure and to insert commercial establishments. Nor would it be acceptable to insert other structures in a mindless attempt at 'urbanising' the vast and magnificent space. As for the missing Governor's Palace, it is really risky to construct a work after the architect's death, there is the likelihood of ending up with a hollow copy. Maybe in fact it is best to keep the Capitol incomplete but develop vegetation beyond the site? (see my Keynote Address). In the course of time as Chandigarh matures, as political tensions decrease, and as tourism becomes a force, the Capitol may well come into its own as a social landscape and supporting festivals and public events. The celebrations on the Capitol in Autumn 2015 revealed such possibilities as did the extraordinary International Yoga day in spring 2016, which saw 30,000 people meditating in unison led by Prime Minister Modi on the great space. Over the next decades it is likely that an urbanised corridor will develop all the way from Agra, through Delhi, up to and beyond Chandigarh, and in the circumstances it would be as well to look upon Chandigarh in its entirety as a welcome low-rise park full of greenery and open space, with the Capitol as a major point of attraction.

No city was built in a day and Chandigarh at half a century is still in its infancy. At all scales of the city it is time to consider what should be preserved long-term and what should be permitted to change. The entire Capitol complex—complete or incomplete—with its surrounding landscapes, including the fields beyond in the direction of the mountains, needs to be protected from the processes of short term commercial and real estate profiteering. Public space, in the 'third world' as elsewhere, is constantly threatened by privatisation.

The Capitol is definitely in the public interest: it is, to refer to an ancient concept, part of *res publica.* As the then President of India, K.R. Narayanan stated at the international conference which took place in the city in 1999, Chandigarh is one of the foundation stones of the modern nation state of India; it even expresses some of the country's basic democratic and secular ideals. The Capitol does not just testify to a particular moment in national history, it is also a place of world importance in the history of architecture, urbanism and landscape art. Even in its present incomplete state it has acquired 'UNESCO World Heritage' status to safeguard it. Through his extraordinary process of invention and transformation, Le Corbusier created something reaching well beyond the scope of his own references and his own time. Dense in meaning, powerful in its forms, it aspires towards universality. The Capitol in Chandigarh is a symbolic landscape which has gradually separated itself from its creator and original context and which now moves on towards an unknown future.

THE INDIAN INCARNATION

B.V. Doshi

I am happy to recount my trepidations while I was learning under Le Corbusier, my mentor and guru, with whom I spent four very impressionable years at his studio in Paris and then almost four years at site, supervising and giving needed information to complete the buildings in Ahmedabad. This is where I discovered the essence of what architecture could be. It was our then Prime Minister, Pandit Jawaharlal Nehru, who invited Le Corbusier to design the plan of Chandigarh, the capital city of the new state of Punjab, and fulfill his desire that Chandigarh herald new impetus to break all the shackles imposed by the foreign rulers and rediscover an Indian identity to match our great civilization.

To build for an eventual population of half million people meant a new flexible open-ended approach to planning, designing and constructing buildings as well as visualizing the future, perhaps a facility in contrast to Corbusier's Radiant city. For this chance, implied opportunity, and challenge meant virtue. The Indian situation of a new nation state with frugal resources inherently meant dealing with uncertainty, ambiguity and unexpected revisions in implementations of any conceived plan.

Cities are not built in a day, they take centuries. Life is conceived here and its end merges with the cities, its culture, values and meaning. Stories are written about ancient cities, and so is the story of our civilization. From ancient Babylon, Mohenjo-Daro to Athens, Rome, Paris, London; all these cities tell us stories about their culture, art institutions and values which get embedded in the city. A city's core is its institutions and it is from where the values and meaning of life disseminate. In our history, after Jaipur came Delhi and then occurred Chandigarh. In his book *Discovery of India*, our then Prime Minister, Pandit Jawaharlal Nehru talks about how our own civilization thrived over centuries and how a new way of life was discovered; Chandigarh was conceived to break from the lethargic past. Nehru must have taken the opportunity to take advantage of Punjab's entrepreneurship and spirituality which gave us this most modern contemporary city of Chandigarh. Though the Post-Independent Punjab is a small state in the Indian subcontinent, he saw in it a new state, imparting value giving, not only to India but also the world; a new contemporary magnet which could attract visitors from all over the world comparable to the virtues of Paris, Rome, New York. A new world where one could experience advanced lifestyle, employment, learning and having the spirit of unity of heart, body and soul; where every being will have a place to nourish family, an opportunity to work, a place everyone could learn, grow, enjoy and have good life besides fresh air and breath. A city where there is no strife, no want and a choice where institutions pursue their beliefs, faith and culture.

To achieve this, he sent his emissaries to hunt for an architect, planner who had vision, skill and reputation and conceive a new way of life for India. It is this search that found Le Corbusier, Maxwell Fry, Jane Drew and Jeanneret. It is important to note that there is no one I know, but Le Corbusier, whose ideal was Michelangelo, one of the greatest artist-architects of the Renaissance. Following this ideal vision, Corbusier in his most mature years, not only conceived the plan of the city of Chandigarh and gave us another city equal to Maharaja Jai Singh's Jaipur, which was a great city created by our famous statesman, politician, astronomer, poet and philosopher. It was in Jaipur that our astronomical beliefs were built at a large scale to express our symbolic connections with galaxies. Likewise, today we see how Le Corbusier not only gave us the symbol of a new city complex, the High Court, the Assembly building, the Secretariat and the Governor's Palace (yet unbuilt) with a new revolutionary concept combining our cultural values to fulfill the mandate of the newly acquired independence. He recognized that the only way to create values is through democratic process. Corbusier, in his four major seminal buildings namely the Assembly Hall, High Court, Secretariat and

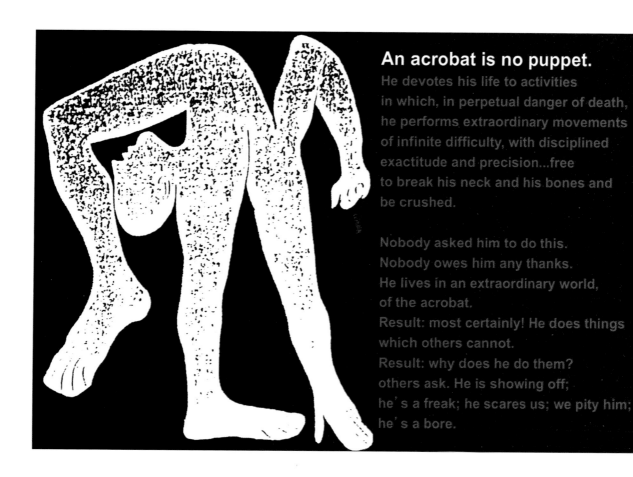

An acrobat is no puppet.

He devotes his life to activities
in which, in perpetual danger of death,
he performs extraordinary movements
of infinite difficulty, with disciplined
exactitude and precision...free
to break his neck and his bones and
be crushed.

Nobody asked him to do this.
Nobody owes him any thanks.
He lives in an extraordinary world,
of the acrobat.
Result: most certainly! He does things
which others cannot.
Result: why does he do them?
others ask. He is showing off;
he's a freak; he scares us; we pity him;
he's a bore.

The acrobat by Le Corbusier
© VastuShilpa Foundation

Governor's Palace, eliminated plinths, steps or levels between the citizens and the decision makers; not only did he do this but in his Master Plan he provided a unique, most unusual, and a rare feature of giving a green valley where every individual, poor or rich, busy or idle could spend time in silence amongst trees and parks, where he could not only cultivate his body, but also connect his soul. He devised ways for the citizen to have opportunities to work, exploit his or her skill and also proposed them frugally, judiciously, and designed a habitat and place to forge a community. Today we see this unique plan and how most satisfaction of life can be had. One of the most important ways of planning this city was to devise a transport network and his seven different scale routes have hierarchical values and allow free flow of traffic. Not only did he plan this, but he also gave us the chance to view everyday our unique natural asset, the Shivalik Hills and the distant Himalayas, a true city worthy of our ancient tradition and culture of which we read references in the Upanishads (ancient Indian treatises) and *Mahabharata*. Today I wish this legendary and visionary architect Le Corbusier was with us to celebrate his creation; we salute him. Though these experiences that I mention, how does one look at them in reality and how do we measure why and how he designed the buildings the way he did and therefore the title of my essay is the 'Indian Incarnation', because I thought that what he was before in Paris and what he was still in Paris, he was not the same in India, particularly in case of architecture in Chandigarh and Ahmedabad.

For example, Le Corbusier expresses his thoughts about an acrobat as if himself,

> An acrobat is no puppet. He devotes his life to activities in which, in perpetual danger of death, he performs extraordinary movements of infinite difficulty, with disciplined exactitude and precision, free to break his neck and his bones and be crushed.

That's how he lived his life. Then he says,

> Nobody asked him to do this. Nobody owes him any thanks. He lives in an extraordinary world, of the acrobat. Result: most certainly! He does things which others cannot. Result: why does he do them? others ask. He is showing off; he is a freak; he scares us; we pity him; he's a bore.

Corbusier in his early travels spent maximum time at the Acropolis in Athens. He was fascinated not only by the location of buildings, the location of the site but also the location and the scale the buildings have, magnificent scale, vast and dignified. Then he writes in his diary that this structure is the same as a wooden column structure in the ancient homes, but here they are made in marble and of a very high scale of great importance. The virtue lies in the transformation.

Before Corbusier arrived in Chandigarh, he had met P.L. Varma, the Chief Engineer of the Chandigarh project, who ultimately became his very close friend and supporter. They both often wondered what could be done and how they could realize his direction of Chandigarh. On this occasion let us remember Mr P.L. Varma and his contribution to the making of Chandigarh.

During all those years that I was in Paris, I had a chance to stay in 'La Maison du japon', on the third floor from where every morning I had the good fortune to have *darshan* (divine sighting) of another of Le Corbusier's public landmarks the Pavilion Suisse Hostel for students, at the 'Cite Universite', full of glass on one side and solid wall on the other. Every day I marvelled at the character and wondered how Le Corbusier expressed his main theory of free ground floor and garden terraces on the top. The glass curtain wall makes the heavy mass disappear.

I saw many sketches in his diaries constantly working his thoughts on 24 hours' cycle of the day, and how the sun would move during summer and winter and how the seasons react. Such drawings and studies helped him to orient his buildings, connect them to the nature and devise means to protect as well as open. Likewise, he was fascinated by the minimum objects that everybody lived with in India.

Le Corbusier's sketches of the cycles of the moon and the Sun, a *charpai* (a cot) and birds flying
©FLC-ADAGP

A *charpai* (Indian cot), he mentioned as a multipurpose object used to sleep, to carry, to make a shade, to store our stuff below. And so are the cycles of the moon. How often he mentioned these cycles of the moon, sun and the birds flying.

One day he told me, while drawing the section of the Mill Owners Building, how the birds would fly through the building and he sketched them on both sides and this is how he looked at life and the buildings he created.

Fascinated, he went around Punjab and saw the villages and sketched those horns of the bulls and the mud walls. Grace is always possible in very simple materials, it's the question of how does one do it.

In 1951, when he visited Ahmedabad he saw this building under construction, designed by Kanvinde for Ahmedabad Textile Industry and Research Association (ATIRA) and discovered the partially sagging concrete slab due to steel shuttering and perhaps called it 'The *Beton Brute*'.

He saw how the workers at site managed to carry on their heads frugal local materials and how simple technologies can work in tandem with his designs.

Simultaneously when he saw the Muslim or Hindu buildings, in summer and in winter, and then the overhangs, temporary ones, he sketched them and then said 'This is how architecture has to be'. For a person who came from Paris, who talked about technology, who talked about Radiant City, who talked about the population in large numbers and living in a sky scraper 20-storeys high saw these things and wondered how should one design? He was a warrior at heart and found ways to win his battles.

For example, we see in the image, Le Corbusier, the warrior with a hat, and on the left you'd see the sketches and his strategy. A Don Quixote looking at the windmill and thinking as if he has to fight the general, so one must learn to fight. The second is the Trojan Horse where you have to have the skills to find ways and means to win the war and the third a horse carriage with a donkey and thus every day you have to work hard and that's what Corbusier was, as expressed in his personal sketch.

Corbusier's philosophy of life is very beautifully expressed in this drawing he presented to Heidi Weber. He saw himself as Don Quixote, who must cultivate the habit of fighting the negative forces and thoughts, and to achieve his goal, including use of Trojan Horses, he must use

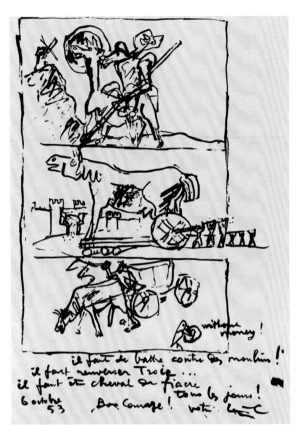

without money !

il faut de battre contre des moulins !
il faut renverser Troie ...
il faut être cheval de fiacre
6 octobre   Bon Courage ! tous les jours !
53   votre Le C

dans le sac de sa peau,
faire ses affaires à soi
et dire merci au Créateur

Le Corbusier

all his shrewdness, skill and ingenuity. And finally, never forget to work incessantly like a cart donkey.

In another drawing, of hands, he talked about hands as God's unique gift. The hands, a very flexible tool, are precisely like a machine and have the intelligence to give and take. That is why the hand has become an extremely important symbol to him. He used to say that there are no permanent traditions, nor any rules that cannot be changed because it is our own inner being that makes them. And with skill, experience and dexterity we can find solutions that are appropriate.

His sketches of Chandigarh show how he began to devise the Sector plan, the details as well as the large plan. One day he sent me a card where he expresses two ideas, collaborations by putting all hands together and on the left he writes *'Dans le sac de sa peu, faire les affaires a soi et dire merci au createur'* which means 'In the sack of your skin, do all the affairs and say thank you to the Creator'. This is what he was constantly advising me and teaching me.

I often noticed while interacting how much he believed that there was somebody, somewhere, who was creating or sending messages so that they could be implemented by him as His instrument. He often referred to the river, which internally connected the source and the destination of the water and where the creator guided it to.

My initial job began with the drawing of the sections of the High Court and when I was drawing, I could not understand the sense of scale. One day suddenly he came, sat on my table, and drew a human figure and he said *'Do you see, when you draw a human figure you will understand what scale is'*. I had never seen such demonstration before, the High Court with such heights, and it is here that I began to learn his way of teaching sitting next to me.

Visiting Chandigarh, I saw this foyer, the main hall of the High Court and then I realized, that not only it denotes—height, but also the way a grand portico is created with its inclined roof and the curvature at the ceiling near the sky. He sketched the detail for me, I remembered then, how I need to learn design and how to merge the surrounding within the inner spaces and how to juxtapose the delicacy and vastness.

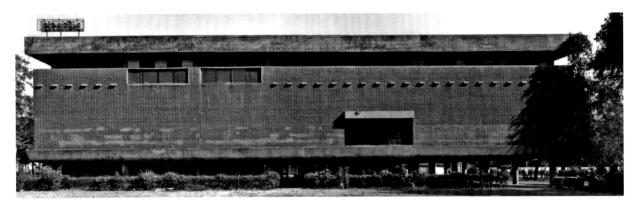

Sanskar Kendra, Ahmedabad
© VastuShilpa Foundation

Few years ago, I went again to Chandigarh and I remembered those scales and then I took some pictures and those pictures reminded me this story, not only about the scale, but about of the relationship between the walls their rounded edges and the kind of space that they created.

When you wander through these buildings, and when you walk from the rear entrance and then come towards the front and look over the assembly, you realize the scale of this building and its relationship to the Assembly building.

Next to my table at Corbusier's studio, it was Michel, a colleague, who was working on the Sarabhai House, on a completely opposite domestic scale. I found that the walls that he was drawing were not only parallel walls but there was also the vault, the Spanish Catalonian arch, made of brick and I wondered how could he work on these two scales at the same time. There were many foreigners, working in the office, each one with a different project and each one had a different building but of totally different scales. I wondered how he managed to work simultaneously on several scales and yet hold their ground.

One day he came and sat on Michel's board and saw the section of the Sarabhai house and then he took a paper and drew the façade of the Sarabhai house. It did not have the vault. It had concrete panels including the parapet and the building looked as if it were a box with concrete panels on the same surface. Coming back, I saw the difference between inside and outside, a totally different experience, subtle contradictions.

Those parallel walls were not in line. They were parallel, at the same distance, but they had staggered openings. Never did I realize that by staggering those, one had another sense of space and lightness. The walls almost disappeared under those heavy beams. Similar was the case with the museum in Ahmedabad. Masogier was working on it and he said that a brick cavity wall is a climatic control device. The museum was provided with internal light and insulation through a double roof where all the services are located. Thereafter he added troughs to the walls for growing creepers.

What he was trying to do was a box on pilotis so that the breeze can come from below, disappear through the courtyards and create a green box. In fact, while the building was about to be completed, the citizens in Ahmedabad asked me questions, 'What kind of a box is this?' and I could not answer them because there was nothing but pure experience. On the rooftop he had proposed hydroponics. We are talking today of sustainability, of green buildings, and he had already proposed them in the 1950s, a totally conscious building expressing temperature and climate.

You can see in the structure, a vertical joint brick wall as if it's a solid box surrounded by a courtyard and thin columns.

Similarly, in the Mill Owners Building, when I first drew the plans, he brought me one cover of a yellow file. On that there was a thumbnail sketch showing an inclined surface line then a box and on the left, he said 'road' and on the right, he said 'river' and the programme that hardly mentioned four offices, etc. Then he said *'Here is the project, do it,'* and when I did the drawing and made a perspective, then the story actually began.

The Mill Owners Building was facing the river on one side and on the other side the road was directly facing east–west. He took the plan and with few changes made a radical departure. Except the two walls which were parallel, facing the boundaries and the open space between the road and the river, the remainder changed totally because he changed the plan. He created a slightly different plan with one wall curved and then the space appeared to be completely open, which I didn't realize then. Eventually when the sun breakers were added, vertical at right angles on the east side, and on the west side we had them inclined, deep, they looked very different and he wanted to make that ramp a royal entrance. A lower entry on the ground floor was made so that you could sneak inside as if it was inferior and where the ramp entered it had double-storeyed height.

So suddenly I discovered, while the building was under construction, that this building is a non-building, completely open, from where you see the sky, you see the birds which he drew, and the river, etc. The room disappears, because there is a relationship between the open and enclosed space. You see this in the section and in the plan, how these devices were made.

A decade ago, I decided to study Corbusier's buildings and find out how they were made; what was the reason. And slowly I discovered, that these are all separate elements put together as if they respond to each element responding to a specific condition giving them a particularity. Particularity in a sense that the roof, the sun breakers, the walls, everything is separate and yet it is together. When I had made that grid, he changed two walls and he made them into one surface and added an elevator and the ramp. There was a vertical wall and you entered by shifting your axis.

Similarly, when I asked him about toilets, he said *'Oh'* and *'you remind me of toilets, very good,'* and then he drew the circle there and the toilets were added.

So, he was constantly trying to find out, how to create virtue out of calamities.

Auditorium at Mill Owners
Building, Ahmedabad
© VastuShilpa Foundation

When it was the hall that we had to design, because I did not know French, to explain he drew those things with colour pencils and crayons and then he started telling me that look, how does a visitor come, then he would make the dots and he would say that you go like this and this and this and this and gradually now we enter inside. Then he drew that curvature because before, few months before, when he had asked me to make the drawing of the hall, he said you know better, and walked away. When I had started drawing I did not know what to do, so I asked Corbusier what was he saying; even he could not explain to me but later he drew this. Then one column which came inside the hall, he made that a stage and said:

> You know in the hall people come but some people don't want to know, they don't want to go there but they would like to find out who is speaking.

Therefore he drew a small window near the entrance, so you could peep in and see who is the speaker and whether you would like to stay there.

And if you don't like it or you don't know what you want, then you would enter inside and then you would not go and sit in the front but you would sit with the chairs in the back. Then he drew the chairs in a row and then drew some chairs at the back and he said you can disappear. What he was all the time talking about was behaviour, human psychology and choice. I think architecture is not just a building. Architecture is not just telling you to do this and do this, but it is a way how architecture acts as a living organism.

Quality of light and variation in light conditions and the various speeds and directions in which the breeze would flow in, I think nobody thinks about them. When you walk in you are suddenly exposed to the interior space and then you feel the breeze and notice the light quality, which is very unusual and very specific. When you go on the first floor the light quality is of another kind. Here you will experience few spaces, for example, a concrete wall and a brick wall which are plastered with a little gap, a vertical slit, not because of the change of material, but the kind of light one would get. While designing the auditorium, the roof was initially flat like the terrace and he said, 'Yes, this room below is dark so how will we get light?', then saying, 'Oh! You know there is a way. Let's change the angles, lift the roof up.' And he lifted the roof on two sides, creating a curvature underneath, almost like a segment that you see in the design for the roof of the Governor's Palace at the Capitol Complex, Chandigarh. That segment really created completely different light conditions. Today you see in this hall, the light penetrating inside and every time the sun changes, shadows change, the light quality changes and to add another dimension to this, the panelling was made inclined so that one would almost feel as if one was dizzy. Incidentally in the beginning the hall was hardly ever occupied because people said they feel dizzy.

There were many ways that he was playing the game. Architecture was a serious game for him but it's a game of learning, acquiring, enjoying and experiencing. Not solid but porous. Porosity was his strength. The building may look solid on one side but porous on the other; some places transparent, and that is what you see in this Mill Owners Building. You see this building on the east side, it's completely fluid and on the west side it is semi-solid and north and south with the blank brick wall completely solid. Through all those devices in the same building you begin to see how he could subtly devise means to create a building which responds to climate

Facing page above:
Sketches of Corbusier's buildings at Ahmedabad © VastuShilpa Foundation

Facing page below:
Sketches of Corbusier's buildings at Capitol Complex, Chandigarh © VastuShilpa Foundation

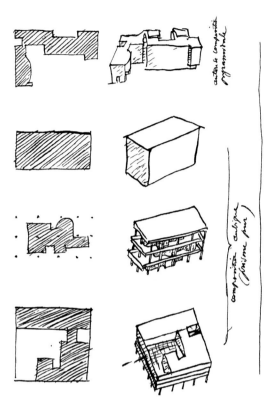

SARABHAI HOUSE

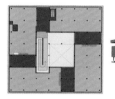

SANSKAR KENDRA

MILLOWNERS ASSOCIATION

VILLA SHODHAN

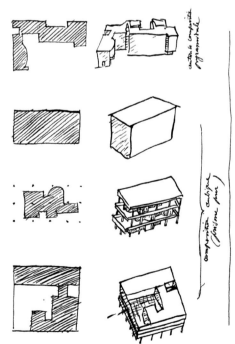

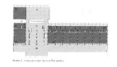

HIGH COURT

ASSEMBLY

GOVERNOR'S PALACE

as if it is conversing with you, it is conversing with the sun, it is conversing with the river, it is conversing with shadow and if you go there in the evening or afternoon the constant changing of the sun's position creates a completely dramatic view of the building. Incidentally, Frank Gehry called me one afternoon and he said, 'I am just coming to Ahmedabad, will you be there?' I said, 'Yes.' He said, 'Come to the Mill Owners Building.'

And as he came there and entered he said, 'This is the "Fountainhead of Architecture" and I have come to pay my homage.' In another hour he left.

Another thing that I discovered is that if you put together the Mill Owners Building facades along with the sketch of the terraces, the Indian paintings drawings with their terraces with people in the balcony, etc., you discover that the Shodhan House is another story.

I presume he was constantly trying to find different ways to express himself. For example, terraces and balconies were always used. Today

Assembly building at Capitol Complex, Chandigarh
© VastuShilpa Foundation

Facing page:
Jantar Mantar at Jaipur by Maharaja Jai Singh
© VastuShilpa Foundation

with all the glass we don't get balconies, we don't get verandas and we get minimum terraces. But in our real life, these are the areas that we use and these are the areas which we cherish. They are not only healthy but better, rather than having air conditioned rooms, and having the same air re-circulated. So here are the four different ways of treating external surfaces and relating them to lifestyle.

Ten years ago, I began to ponder about how Corbusier's mind worked; the way he could manage to get such diverse work, specific yet unique and indirectly expressing the place, the content, the climate and the lifestyle.

That was the time I also realized how the Indian miniature paintings were done on only one page, i.e. one miniature representing the whole story and that made me look into Corbusier studies and suddenly I found that in 1929 when he wrote his *Complete Works* (*Oeuvre Complete*), he wrote about his four principles, A meandering house, a cube, a freeform and one which was perforated and porous, I analyzed these four buildings in Ahmedabad and I discovered how they were fitting together in the Indian context and his Indian projects. That is why I called this essay Corbusier's reincarnation.

While analyzing his four Indian projects at Chandigarh: The Secretariat, the High Court, the Assembly, and the Governor's Palace, once again, these theories begin to appear which are of consequence, and I was happy to know that Corbusier deep inside had his own theories. But normally we don't talk about them and neither do we study them when we study the work of Le Corbusier.

For example, if you look at the High Court building and the Assembly building you will see these juxtapositions: form, structure, articulation and scale. The Assembly building has the portico exactly in the right angles to the surface and not in the horizontal direction at all as if the supports, the vertical walls don't exist and in the assembly the roof has the revised version of the cooling tower with a symbolic gesture to instruments of light, sun, etc., as if it's a magical place. I think the Assembly is where the public takes decisions, the leadership talks about vision, talks about challenges, talks about a new world and that is how one must look at the way buildings are made, even in their juxtaposition, even their relationship.

Facing page:
Corbusier with the model of the roof of the Assembly building
© VastuShilpa Foundation

Model of Governor's
Palace at Chandigarh
© VastuShilpa Foundation

When I had gone to Chandigarh, I saw this model of the roof of the Assembly building. At that time the roof was not constructed. So I requested Corbusier that why don't you hold it in your hands and then you sit on the chair and you would look like a tribal chief. He was amused. He said 'Ok let's take a picture,' and it is that picture, and next

to that you will see the Assembly roof. Below that you will discover the Yantra, designed and created by Maharaja Jai Singh in his astronomical laboratory at Jaipur and this is where I found Corbusier's connections to history, to knowledge and to eternity as those of the Maharaja Jai Singh and I salute both of them for these great revelations.

Again, in the façade, in the roof or the interiors of all these buildings everything is different but of the same significance. For example, in the Assembly building's roof and the columns in the foyer where all the parliamentarians meet, there is only, mushroom-like capital, the ceiling is dark, yet it has beautiful light. Actually, if the roof was not there, you would have said it is an Indian chowk. It is a gathering place and what he created is really an enclosed space, sufficiently illuminated and yet giving. And there you will see that the room which is added was added subsequently. So he had no problems of additions, he had no problems of finding alternatives. His was the way of constantly incorporating the emerging additions as if it was a painting, and he the painter, the artist, the sculptor.

It is an impossible task to use a cooling tower which is a drab geometrical and very function specific form, yet Le Corbusier created his Assembly with this object. Circular, in form, but his way of placing those acoustical panels changed the entire imagery.

When you walk towards the Assembly, you first see the portico from far away and then experience it walking beneath it as an alley. It is one of the most significant buildings, and the most significant thing to remember is that like all Renaissance architects or historical architects or painters who created their own entrance door which talks of their philosophy and what they believed in, the Assembly door too has a similar significance.

In the Capitol Complex he must have thought that it isn't necessary to be detached if we are making decisions or when we give justice, (of course that's my view) though the plaza is there, there also have to be other places with different uses, including public participation. It is like Fatehpur Sikri where there are lot of empty spaces. No doubt it has a different scale, this is what 'I' think he must have had thought of, because I had personally asked this question to him when Dr Gideon told me that Le Corbusier said that Piazza San Marco is the greatest living room in the

Facing page above left:
Corbusier with his
model maker
© VastuShilpa Foundation

Facing page above right:
Corbusier with model of a hand
© VastuShilpa Foundation

Facing page below:
Corbusier in front of the
Secretariat, Chandigarh
© VastuShilpa Foundation

world, whereas the Assembly and other buildings are his homage to the Himalayas and the hills.

Unfortunately, the Governor's Palace is still not built, but I think it is essential that the vacant place must be filled. It must be given for a public cause, if not only for administrative purposes and I think it would be a good idea if there is a competition to design this building. However, I think, we must take care that the profile that has been formed by Le Corbusier of the Governor's Palace is still retained. Corbusier always attached significance to the palm. For him it was the Open Hand to give and share and to talk and we in India also talk about the palm, and the open hand is for giving blessings and this is what it represents here. Incidentally his dealings with staff members were very friendly and in this case, you would see in the photograph, where his craftsman who did all his models was there and he always chatted with him, and learned from him and that way again the use of scale.

He always believed that you cannot be living in isolation, you may meditate in isolation, may search for yourself, but you must work in collaboration.

These are the pictures that I took of Corbusier in front of the Secretariat. We are talking of Chandigarh, and Chandigarh of tomorrow, and I've put this photograph which I had taken at the time when I came back. I believe his vision on many issues needs to be resolved in the changing circumstances. For example, how do you deal with such wide roads, what do you do with the Sectors which have no connections, etc. One of the ways to do it is to think about it a fresh at a much larger scale and give people glimpses of both earlier and tomorrow's visions through new institutions and facilities.

The Assembly mural door I mentioned was done in enamel; and created by Le Corbusier himself in Paris with symbols of Health, Wisdom and Life. You can see the solar movements, the moon, the trees, the goat, the animals, the serpents, everything is there. So, I think he is telling us that don't look at architecture as exclusive, make it inclusive, be a part of nature and be connected to them so that you would learn to be flexible yet integrated.

LE CORBUSIER AND THE QUESTION OF BRUTALISM

Jacques Sbriglio

'The styles are a lie. Style is a unity of principle that animates all the works of an era and results from a distinctive state of mind.

Our era fixes its style every day.
Our eyes, unfortunately, are not yet able to discern it.'

—Le Corbusier
Towards a New Architecture

As you can see in this quote from *Towards a New Architecture*, Le Corbusier has never been at ease with the question of style in architecture. It seemed to him that the notion of style referred back to an architecture of the past, and therefore could not be applied to modern architecture.

Yet now that his body of work is finite, there is an undeniable 'Le Corbusier style' that still influences many architects today.

I would argue that there are two styles rather than one. A first one, from the 1922–1928 era, that others named *Purism*. A second one, from 1930 to 1965 (subtracting a few years for war), that we can call *Brutalism*. Historians tend to argue that the emergence of this 'New Brutalism' dates back to, in the case of Le Corbusier, the construction of the Unité d'Habitation in Marseilles. In reality, its origins are rooted in the early

1930s when he moved away from modern architecture dogmas, even if he contributed to their elaboration.

This distinction is, in fact, critical re-evaluation, rather that renouncement. It is a time for Le Corbusier where he attempts to do two things: first, establishing new relationships between tradition and modernity. Then, making architecture progress through a drift from theory to poetry.

The results were spectacular. No more purist architectures and their abstractions, no more rational volumetric plays from Euclidian geometry. It was time for improbable encounters of volumes in space, curvatures or odd shapes, time for material surprises and colors to resonate with raw concrete, the infamous 'béton brut'.

When I designed the exhibition in Marseilles in 2013, I was interested in the origins of this Brutalist 'style' in Le Corbusier's work. He himself defined this Brutalism as 'clumsy romanticism', referring partly to the flaws and

Facing page above:
The ramp and *brise soleil* of the Mill Owners Building
© FLC-ADAGP

Facing page below:
The enamelled door of the Assembly
© Rajiv Kumar

The interior of the main assembly chamber
© Rajiv Kumar

defects in the construction of the Unité d'Habitation in Marseilles. It seems appropriate to remind ourselves of this well-known extract, from the opening of the inauguration speech:

> A way of dealing with the worst blemish of the Unité at Marseilles, which is the handrail of the ramp which runs up to the children's rest room on the roof, has occurred to me. I have decided to make beauty by contrast. I will find its complement and establish a play between crudity and finesse, between the dull and intense, between precision and accident.

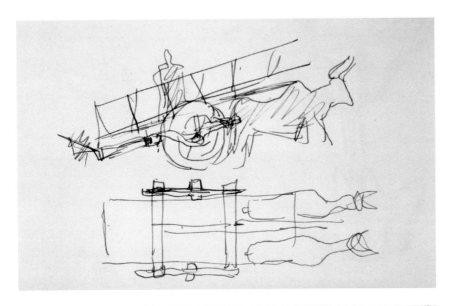

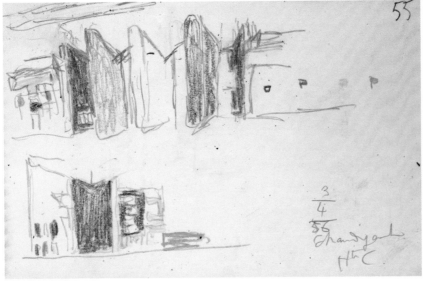

Left and facing page: Some elements of inspiration for Brutalism as reflected in Le Corbusier's architecture.

Select images identified by editors, as associated with Jacques Sbriglio's presentation at the Symposium.

© FLC-ADAGP

This quote is crucial as it demonstrates how, despite his usual distance from construction sites, Le Corbusier acknowledges these 'accidents' as integral parts of his aesthetics and his work. Which, by the way, does not make restoration an easy task!

Coming back to the origins of his Brutalist positioning, I suggest we mainly look into the following directions.

First, the everlasting fascination of Le Corbusier for nature, both in its geomorphic and cosmic dimensions. He considered nature, man, and architecture, three intricate and non-dissociable elements of a project. Second, the ambivalence between his attraction for industrial rationality and his idealization of craft.

Then, his passion for both grand historical works of architecture, and vernacular architecture.

Additionally, his discovery of primitive arts and *art brut*, particularly through his cousin Louis Soutter's drawings.

Finally, his undying love for the Mediterranean, a place for ancestral cultures with the note-worthy presence of Greece and the Parthenon in the origins of architecture.

Administration building, Panjab University, Chandigarh
Photo courtesy: Le Corbusier Centre, Chandigarh

This is how, between 1945 and 1965, that is exactly 20 years, Le Corbusier delivered around 20 Brutalist *chefs-d'oeuvres*, in a magnificent unity of thinking. I want to stress here the importance of this *unity*, as these works stand today as major figures of the 20th century global architectural landscape.

These *chefs-d'oeuvre*, that I will provocatively designate as *post-modern*, question (just like numerous prototypes) the programs they were invited to solve, whether it be individual collective housing, a chapel, a convent, a museum, a hospital, or even a palace. In this objective, they set up audacious composition systems in plan, sections and façades. They attempt to mix construction technologies ranging from the most archaic to the most sophisticated, to finally establish astonishing relationships between all disciplines of the arts, what Le Corbusier called *la synthèse des arts,* or the 'artistic symbiosis'. These systems contributed to the development of new images and imposed a new way of thinking architecture in the light of its most essential component: poetry.

LE CORBUSIER'S IMPRINT

INDIA AND BEYOND

LE CORBUSIER REDIRECTED
A brief history of his influence in Venezuela

Alfredo Brillembourg

His elevation transfigures him into a voyeur. It puts him at a distance. It transforms the bewitching world by which one was 'possessed' into a text that lies before one's eyes.*

Le Corbusier was an architect and a thinker whose influence is felt all around the world. His work here, in a post-partition India, is one of his most palpable visions, one of the rare instances in his career where he himself was able to realize an urban-scale vision. His designs and attempts were numerous, from his early *Ville Radieuse* proposal for Paris to his Unités in Berlin and Marseille, to unrealized plans for Algiers, Barcelona, and elsewhere. And even more, he served as much as an educator and as an inspiration to a younger generation through his personal relationships and his leadership in Congrès Internationaux d'Architecture moderne (CIAM). While he never designed for Venezuela, where our office was founded, we came of age as architects in a world he helped design.

In 1929 Corbusier came to South America to lecture in Argentina. He recounts the trip in his book *Precisions*, a book which has been foundational in our careers. In it, he writes about a flight from Buenos Aires to Asunción, Paraguay. Flying over the great Paraná river, he 'saw spectacles. They could qualify themselves as cosmic, an invitation to meditation, something that calls for the fundamental things of our Earth.'

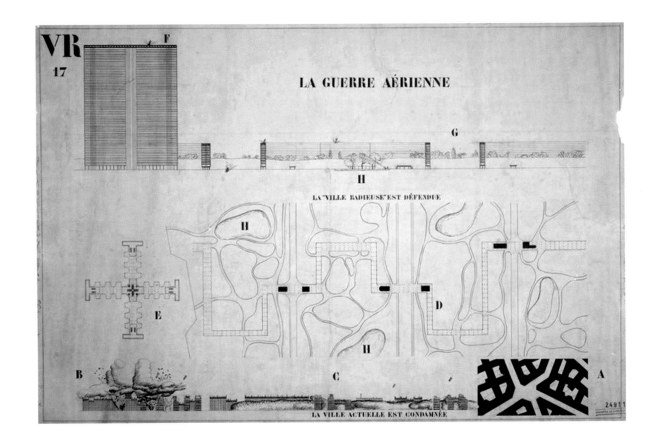

From the privileged position of the aerial view—something at that time still quite rare even for politicians, much less architects—he floated over the broad meanders of the pampas, and considered it both something inspirational and to be built upon. He sketched a plan for a great metropolis on that river, which, while never realized in his time, bears a strong resemblance to Puerto Madero, the present day port of Buenos Aires. His trip left him very hopeful that Argentina and Brazil were ideal countries for modern architecture. In his lifetime, though, all of his efforts resulted in only two works in the Americas, Villa Curutchet in Argentina and the Carpenter Centre at Harvard. But his influence was nonetheless felt, through the legacy of young architects who worked with him, included Rogelio Salmona in Colombia, Teodoro González de León in Mexico, and of course Oscar Niemeyer and Lúcio Costa in Brazil. I would like to talk to you today about a big inspiration for Urban-Think Tank (U-TT), Carlos Raul Villanueva, the great Modernist architect of Caracas and of Venezuela.

There isn't any proven direct connection between Villanueva and Corbusier, though it's likely that they did cross paths in Europe, where

Carpenter Centre, Cambridge,
Massachusetts
© Rajnish Wattas

Villanueva was educated and where he encountered CIAM. But the lineage is clear through Niemeyer, his contemporary and an architect he knew well. Indeed, his great works, like the Ciudad Universitaria of the Universidad Central de Venezuela in Caracas, or the housing projects at El Silencio and 23 de Enero clearly represent an architecture inspired by both Corbusier and Niemeyer.

The University—where U-TT once taught, years after its construction—displays Villanueva's capacity to plan and design institutions at an urban scale, as Corbusier did here in Chandigarh. He drew up both the axial urban plan and some of the initial buildings in the early 1940s, not so long before Chandigarh. Villanueva's engagement with the University's development, however, would last through 1960. What's really interesting to us is how his plans develop over that time, how his original, very rationalist architecture and circulation scheme develop into something far more fluid.

Villanueva said in 1967 that 'architecture is a social act, par excellence. A utilitarian art.' This speaks volumes about the evolving designs

for the Ciudad Universitaria, where a sort of Tendenza architecture becomes liberated, becomes criss-crossed with covered walkways that meander throughout the campus and join the buildings together. La Plaza Cubierta, as its called, becomes a place where people hold dance classes, a space into which professors extend their lectures. It becomes a really fabulous space, and an intensely social space as well. It's listed as a UNESCO world heritage site alongside Corbusier's work in Chandigarh.

While Corbusier's architectural work here did not include the construction of any examples of his well-known Unités d'Habitation, that project and the project here are closely linked. The Unité in Marseille was completed as construction of the Secretariat building here was still in progress. That building, and its later iterations in France and Germany directly influenced Villanueva's major housing projects in Caracas, most famously 23 de Enero, or 23rd of January. This was a major project of architecture and urban design, and one that was in a sense the end of the rationalist project in Venezuela.

Facing page above and below:
Villa Curutchet, Argentina
© FLC-ADAGP

Universidad Central de
Venezuela in Caracas
© Daniel Schwartz/U-TT

The housing project, a landscape of 38 superblocks on a hilly site, represented a forceful housing effort by the then-dictator Marcos Pérez Jiménez. Villanueva at that time was working for a government that was capable of bulldozing slums and replacing them with international style towers. But when that government fell, in 1958, the poor people who were removed from the land rushed in and not only occupied the apartments within the buildings, but the open, reserved land between them as well. People flocked into the blocks, and as their friends and family members arrived, they created a secondary urbanism, one that infiltrated and plugged into the housing blocks.

This informal growth is a phenomenon that has long fascinated our office, and its something that you can conceptualize as an alternative Modernism. Not only that, but an alternative that can coexist: formal infrastructure with informal urbanism. It's something that we've studied in India, though never here in Chandigarh, where I understand that Corbusier's designs perhaps led to informal growth in some ways here, and there's certainly a relationship between Modernism and slums that's very interesting. You can see it as well on the edges of Brasilia, as has been well documented. What separates Caracas in some senses is simply the proximity of the two cities.

We have argued for a long time that there is a direct linkage between Corbusier and the architecture of informality. His Domino House, designed in 1914 as a housing prototype meant to respond to a wartime Europe, epitomizes flexibility, the open plan, and early modern housing as a whole. But it also deeply resembles the architecture of the *ranchos* or *barrios*—the informal neighborhoods—in Caracas. Concrete slabs provide not only a versatile platform for different interior layouts and needs, but also a foundation for further upward growth. This is all to say that we would argue that Corbusier lives on not only in the Modernist towers of Caracas, but in the concrete and brick slums surrounding them as well.

And of course these kinds of growth come with their own problems, but we believe, as the English architect and thinker John Turner wrote in the 1970s, that they offer real value as well. And that takes us to one of our defining principles at U-TT: that the architects of today cannot operate like Le Corbusier. The world today demands that we look for another model. The architect, however, can be a global architect; it's about

Universidad Central de
Venezuela in Caracas
© Daniel Schwartz/U-TT

exchange. If you're not looking at global examples, you're not looking at all. Our coming to India, coming from Caracas, and working in Switzerland and exchanging ideas with all of you is crucial.

Architecture has become too important to be left to just architects. Even Villanueva, a great architect in his time, wasn't able to provide housing to all of his nation's needy people. He brought amazing strategies from his education in Europe to help his native country, and reimagined those strategies for the South American climate and culture, as Niemeyer and others did as well. Corbusier learned from nature and the people during his trip to the Americas, and carried that knowledge back to Europe, just as he adapted his knowledge to India to develop Chandigarh, and absorbed the intelligence here as well.

* Michel de Certean, *The Practice of Everyday Life* (Oakland: UC Press, 1984), p.92.

LE CORBUSIER
Impacting post-Independence Indian architecture

Raj Rewal

We are passing through a critical phase in India when the idealism of the early post-Independence era is being drowned in consumerist and market economy values. Imagine two senior officers from Punjab: P.N. Thapar and P.L. Varma, the former an administrator and the other an engineer, who went to Europe looking for the world's finest architect and town planner around 1950. I would like to pay tribute to them today for their endeavour and idealism for bringing one of the greatest visionary Modernist architects of his time to India. Today these engineers would be hauled up by the authorities for not inviting tenders for the Chandigarh design!

There was a generation of Indian architects who had worked directly along with Le Corbusier in Chandigarh and contributed enormously to his vision. The works of M.N. Sharma, Bhanu Mathur, Aditya Prakash, Jeet Malhotra and many others are an important contribution for the harmonious development of Chandigarh.

Corbusier's impact on young Indian architects who had studied and worked abroad was electrifying. There were long discussions and debates in the 1960s about Chandigarh—whether the city lacked urbanity and was too spread out with long distances. Some had a view that it was a vast suburbia in the name of a Garden City. The concrete frame of Corbusier's structures was universally accepted but the vocabulary of

using concrete as a facing material or outer skin was beginning to be considered problematic in the Indian weather.

Fatehpur Sikri
Photo courtesy: Raj Rewal

Personally, I was influenced by Corbusier's ability to transcend his own considerable design vocabulary to explore an architectural expression for each building. His works, based on rigour and austerity were wrongly termed brutal. In fact, he could be playful, imposing and sublime depending on the building type.

We are living in a period of rapid change. Corbusier's language based on the columns which free the ground under buildings, the free plan, strip windows, *brise soleil*, sun breakers, etc., have become part of the architectural history and they may not be valid today. But there is an aspect of Corbusier's works which draws deeply from Mediterranean Europe's heritage, and other references which evoke deep feelings.

It was the expressive force of Corbusier's architecture that hit me just when I was starting my architectural practice. The metaphors and symbols can be read differently in Corbusier's works but the important lesson for me was that architecture can express diverse feelings; it can be executed in the new language of our time and Modernism need not be sterile. I believe the poetry of his buildings and their spirit or 'rasa' sustained with deep spiritual values in a language of our time would live forever crossing cultural barriers or stylistic fashions.

When I first saw the Assembly building at the Capitol Complex, Chandigarh, I could not help thinking that it reminded me of Reims Cathedral in France which I had seen earlier. I mean these two buildings don't resemble each other at all, but the quality of dark surface with very dim light percolating from the height in the Assembly building evokes the great French Cathedrals, so it is the emotional impact of Corbusier's building which touched me the most.

Now, how to build for contemporary India? Corbusier had shown us one way, so I was searching and very early I began to draw upon the essence of traditional Indian Architecture for my own works. In fact, I was obliged to teach history of Indian architecture and later, in 1986, was a curator of the exhibition on traditional Indian Architecture in Paris, which involved detailed studies of Fatehpur Sikri, Jaisalmer, Datia, Orchha, etc.

My frequent visits to various parts of India allowed me to absorb the rich fabric into which Indian cities had been woven. Cool shadows and air currents through courtyards are built into the grain of the cities. Settlement patterns, which promote the creation of microclimate by diffusing light, are important lessons from the past.

For the last 40–50 years it has been my endeavour to search for an Architectural language, a grammar for contemporary Indian conditions which may have a wider reference. In this context, a few of my works draw upon traditions in an innovative language and some may see Corbusier's underlying spirit here which propelled me to find my own path.

PERMANENT EXHIBITION COMPLEX, HALL OF NATIONS, NEW DELHI 1970–72

The Permanent Exhibition Complex is designed to form the focus of 121 hectares of exhibition ground in New Delhi. The design was evolved to meet the constraints of time, availability of materials and labour, but above all, to reflect symbolically and technologically, India's intermediate technology in the 25th year of its independence. The space frame structure in concrete demonstrates the use of labour intensive construction process with state-of-the-art Indian engineering capabilities.

The depth of the structural system was utilised as a sun breaker and conceived in terms of the traditional 'jaali', a geometrical pattern of perforations that serves to obstruct direct rays of the harsh sun while permitting air circulation.

NEHRU PAVILION, NEW DELHI 1972

In 1972, I designed the Nehru Pavilion, a museum to exhibit objects and photographic panels of Jawaharlal Nehru's life and times. While working on the design, I kept in mind the personality of Jawaharlal Nehru, the first prime minister of India, a sensitive intellectual and democrat who

Facing page above:
Hall of Nations interior,
New Delhi
Photo courtesy: Raj Rewal

Facing page below:
Hall of Nations exterior,
New Delhi

Hall of Nations interior,
New Delhi

Photos courtesy: Raj Rewal

would have hated any manifestation of pomposity to honour him. How could a pavilion allow one to symbolize Nehru's life? There were no relevant contemporary prototypes; I began to search deliberately for older models. I had seen Buddhist grass mounds in Nepal that contained relics of the Buddha. Inspired by these, I came upon the idea of grassy embankments enclosing exhibition spaces at two levels. The circulation system for the exhibition was based on *parikrama*—the circumambulatory movement around the central shrine of temples—and the plan began to resemble the Tantric yantras.

NATIONAL INSTITUTE OF IMMUNOLOGY, NEW DELHI 1984–2006

The National Institute of Immunology, New Delhi, a campus dedicated to research, comprising laboratories and housing clusters is influenced by the traditional *havelis*. I carefully studied the manner in which they counter the intense heat of the day by building around courtyards, and then incorporated their underlying principles within the framework of current norms and functional requirements.

The use of community spaces within the campus has affinities with Indian citadels such as Fathehpur Sikri where a group of structures built around interlocking courtyards of varying scales and functions are linked to each other through gateways and shaded paths across enclosures with distant vistas and shifting axes.

LISBON ISMAILI CENTRE, PORTUGAL 1995-2000

The design is influenced by morphology of traditional spatial arrangements as observed in Alhambra in Spain, based on the ideals of a *'paradise garden'*. The façade of the building reinterprets the Islamic patterns in a bold structural system. We have used stone as a basic structural element in conjunction with steel for supporting the roof. The 'Garden of Paradise' occupies a central place in Islamic culture, providing pleasure enhanced by plants and running water.

The doctrine of cosmic unity 'where one is a part of the whole' is central to the Islamic philosophy and spiritual concerns. Islamic art is essentially a way of depicting and discovering this unity through geometrical patterns.

Facing page above:
Nehru Pavillion, New Delhi
Photo courtesy: Raj Rewal

Facing page below:
Institute of Immunology,
New Delhi
Photo courtesy: Raj Rewal

The supporting walls and roof of the Prayer Hall of the Centre are designed as a *jaali* (lattice) in prefabricated natural stone elements which are joined together with epoxy glue and braced with stainless steel members.

LIBRARY FOR THE INDIAN PARLIAMENT NEW DELHI 1989–2003

While designing the new Library for the Indian Parliament 30 years later, I wanted to imbibe and express the deeper concerns of enlightenment as observed in the Jain temple of Ranakpur, Rajasthan, through expression of light or spatial arrangement from Fatehpur Sikri symbolising liberty, but, of course, all in a distinct new language of building.

It was important for me to echo the essential values and not mimic the historic forms and surely this was an important lesson learnt from Corbusier. I felt that abstract values of serenity and enlightenment can be restated in the language of our time in the Library complex.

I had to respond to the urban context of the circular Parliament building as well as the intellectual challenge posed by Edwin Lutyens, the colonial architect of the building. My solution was to design a library complex which resonates with its surroundings, evokes the traditional spirit of enlightenment but is based on modern technology and values of democratic India.

The analogy of a relationship between a Guru and the King may not be far-fetched while comparing the new library with the existing Parliament.

Facing page above:
Lisbon Ismaili Centre, Portugal
Photo courtesy: Raj Rewal

Facing page below:
Lisbon Ismaili Centre, Portugal
Photo courtesy: Raj Rewal

Library for the Indian
Parliament , New Delhi
Photo courtesy: Raj Rewal

STATE UNIVERSITY OF PERFORMING AND VISUAL ARTS, ROHTAK, HARYANA 2008–2014

The Rohtak Visual Arts institutional campus is one of the very important urban complexes to be built in North India after Corbusier's Capitol Complex in Chandigarh. Its four components of fine arts, architecture, film making and fashion design are built around a series of interlinked courtyards dominated by an emblematic structure for the auditorium and library echoing symbolic values from India's historic past. Its slanting circular solar disc on the roof may well recall the Konark Sun Temple's wheel or the dharma chakra from the Buddhist stupas.

The Rohtak Visual Arts complex is built in the traditional material of sandstone recalling the great Mogul monuments and the forts of Rajasthan. The spatial configuration of the courtyards which keep the heat and dust away, creates micro-climate which is another important lesson from Indian precedents.

Facing page and above:
State University of Performing
and Visual Arts, Rohtak
Photo courtesy: Raj Rewal

The campus is visualized as a state-of-the-art University which incorporates the idea of intermingling students studying fine arts, architecture, fashion, television and film making. India has a booming industry related to all the aforementioned disciplines and the campus would be a major centre for students in North India.

These interlinked spaces are defined on two ends by common activity hubs. One of these houses auditoriums on the ground floor, a conference centre on the first floor and a central library on the top-most floor. This circular building with an ascending staircase forms one of the poles of the urban complex.

The roof of the library at the top-most level is covered with a slanting solar disc with photovoltaic panels at 22 degrees to the horizon, to generate maximum solar energy. The ascending staircase around the common activity cylinder has echoes of the parikarma, encircling the Sanchi Stupa, which relates to Buddhist scriptures. The idea of the ascending steps is followed in the monasteries of Bagan in Burma and the famous monument of Borobudur in Indonesia.

I have shared some of my public and institutional works hoping that you would make up your own mind about the impact of Corbusier on my architectural and urban design endeavours. Life in architecture is a long journey and during the last 40 years I have tried to find my own way; but Corbusier's idea that architectural expression has to be sought in a modern language and with structural tools of our time has remained a guiding principle.

However the spaces between the buildings in my works and the grammar of surface treatment is different from Corbusier's sun breakers in concrete. The lessons from tradition are inherent in Corbusier's Assembly building where light and space are given a new life to symbolise secular democracy. The forms of Corbusier's buildings are innovative but they carry deep messages from the past which have lasting impact on contemporary Indian architecture.

Historical references, if you find them in my work, are echoes from the past like the Dharma Chakra from Buddhist tradition in Rohtak University, Mandala diagram in the plan of the Parliament Library, and Islamic patterns as structural elements in the Lisbon Ismaili Centre. It is the essence of *Rasa* of traditional values which permeates the work and illuminates the modern language of structures.

I hope the consumerist culture and the rule of the insensitive bureaucrats and architecturally illiterate building promoters would not curb the creative spirit of Indian architecture, which was certainly triggered by Corbusier's brave new experiment in Chandigarh.

Facing page:
Studies of Open Hand
Photo courtesy:
Le Corbusier Centre

Pp. 88–89:
Yoga Day celebrations at
Capitol Complex, Chandigarh,
on 22 June 2016
Photo courtesy: *The Tribune*

CHANDIGARH'S HERITAGE
IS WORLD HERITAGE

LE CORBUSIER'S CAPITOL
Completing the incomplete

S.D. Sharma

Le Corbusier was a phenomenon of nature, a born genius, an enigma for the world—whom we saw coming every day to office, walking straight to his room, slightly rubbing his heels on the brick tile floor at the end of the smaller block of the Architect's Office building, designed by Pierre Jeanneret, his associate and cousin, whenever he visited Chandigarh, twice a year for a month each time.

I came closer to him to know him better during the opportunity to work with him on his Museum and Art gallery building. It was the rarest opportunity to see the master working and explaining subtleties of architecture and weaving his philosophy about life and architecture in every line he drew. In Chandigarh, he laid stress on the lyricism in architecture in the modern age which can be achieved by use of crystalline geometry, purity, simplicity and order of regulating lines. Chandigarh has become a symbol of Modernism, a Mecca for the world's architects and planners, it is considered that there are yet some hidden treasures in the crust of the land of Chandigarh for which generations of architects and tourists will continue coming to look.

We architects, who had the opportunity to work with him, knew he was compassionate, warm and generous, despite his outwardly stern and upright demeanour. This was my experience while working with him as well.

Just a month before his death he wrote a detailed note regarding his life and works, like a philosophic testament, in which he talks like a monk with prophetic fervour giving a sermon to humanity. He said in that long note,

> Constancy is the definition of life—and to be constant one must be modest with exactitude and precision. It is a mark of inner strength and courage, to confront basic issues of life and there is only one judge i.e. one's own conscience that is yourself and how one can reach from its repellent to the sublime stage depends on each individual.

Le Corbusier in his ideology considered architecture, planning and sculpture as a unique phenomenon of plastic nature in the service of poetic research. Such was the mind of the creator of the city that he laid the foundation on such generic principles that even after more than 65 years, the city is still attractive and addictive.

Chandigarh is a DNA of Modernism, the seed of which was sown by Le Corbusier himself, its lodestar, which he advocated and supported all his life. Chandigarh has all the generic principles and ideology of Modernism and till date it stands as its biggest testimonial in the world.

In order to freeze all that he stood for in life, he selected a site at the helm of the city and called it Capitol Complex, which he described in his own words,

> The Capitol Complex is an admirable park with mountains, trees, flowers, shallow pools and architecture. It is planned to the pedestrian, Man the master of himself on his feet, walking free of fear. Automobiles are prohibited and the land is arranged in 2 levels, a pedestrian plateau at 5 meters and below a level of road and parking. An acropolis of 20th century a crowning glory of Chandigarh.

Here he planned four edifices to enable the Capitol to function as the seat of the government, which was the main reason behind the city to be built, and four monuments to make the place more sacred and incidentally a source of message for humanity. However, one edifice and one monument is not yet built along with a few minor features.

He placed these edifices and monuments on a clean canvas with the help of geometry, golden section and the Modulor. Starting clockwise the Secretariat stands like a boundary on the western side of the complex, then the Assembly, then Tower of Shadows and Geometrical hill close by, then Martyr's memorial, Governor's residence on the extreme northern end (not yet built) then Open Hand and finally the High Court. In this campus, the pattern of all edifices is of rough concrete, the reason for which Le Corbusier explained in his own words,

> May our roughest concrete reveal that, beneath them, our sensibilities are refined and delicate.

1. Assembly Building

2. Secretariat

3. High Court

4. Governor's palace

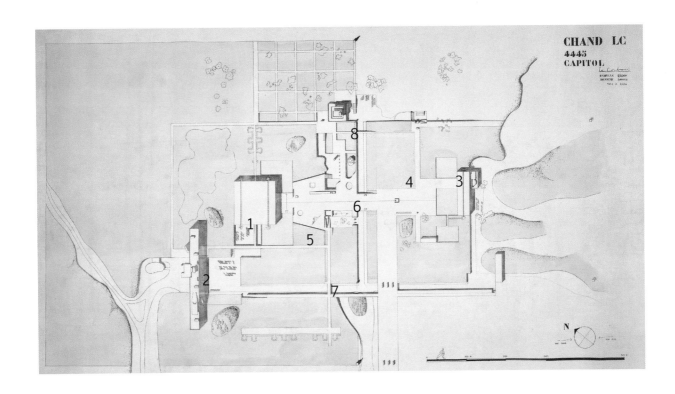

Initial plan of the Capitol Complex, Chandigarh
© FLC-ADAGP

5. Open Hand

6. Tower of shadows

7. Martyr's Memorial

8. Geometrical hill

Photos courtesy: Chandigarh Administration

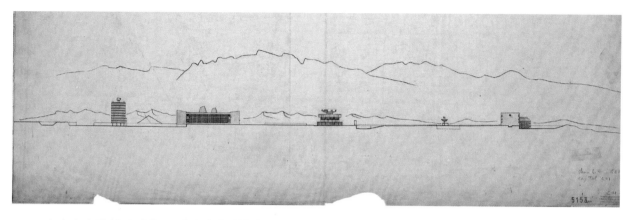

Top:
Initial sketch of the Capitol
Complex, Chandigarh
© FLC-ADAGP

Above:
Secretariat building, Capitol
Complex, Chandigarh
Photo courtesy: Chandigarh
College of Architecture,
Chandigarh

At the very initial stage of planning of Chandigarh, he took the decision to use the concept of Modulor in the city from micro to macro level, which was implemented in totality. He also placed four edifices essential for the Capitol (the seat of the government) in pure geometry, golden section and Modulor dimensions and joined them together with catalytic elements by way of small monuments creating an esplanade surrounded by water bodies, steps, ramps and greenery to create a landscape of breathtaking beauty. However, it is still incomplete. Only two constituents which would have helped to unify the campus are yet to be built.

It is necessary to know all that exists to understand the importance of the missing link.

First is the Secretariat building; it marks the left end of the Capitol Complex and stands as a well-composed image of six blocks separated by

expansion joints, bearing some semblance to the Marseilles Apartments, one of Le Corbusier's projects being built during the same time.

The building has proportions, scale, rhythm, immaculate punctuations, and the ramp outside that reduces the visual length of the building. The most magnificent image in the complex stands next, the Assembly building, which has a very ceremonial portico and the grand door with rich iconography painted by Le Corbusier himself—symbolising the planet with nature of life. On the inauguration day of this door Corbusier said,

> I am intellectual with hands, when I was young engraver of watches.
> Today only the dimensions have changed.

The eight deep columns resemble the Parthenon's eight round columns that fascinated Le Corbusier the most, leaving an indelible impression for all his life. The most capturing are the interiors—serene, impressionable, reminiscent of Gothic architecture or Roman Assembly Halls. Indeed, what Goethe said is true, 'it is here the architecture frozen like music can be experienced.'

Close to this building are the Tower of Shadows and the Geometric hill, both complementing each other. One is abstract and other explains the details. Le Corbusier was so possessed by the sun that he derived most of the vocabulary of architecture from it and valued it intensely. This monument teaches us climatology.

Tower of Shadows, Capitol Complex, Chandigarh
Photo courtesy: Chandigarh College of Architecture, Chandigarh

Above left:
Assembly Building, Capitol Complex, Chandigarh
Photo courtesy: Chandigarh College of Architecture, Chandigarh

Martyr's Memorial, Capitol
Complex, Chandigarh
Photo courtesy: Chandigarh
College of Architecture,
Chandigarh

Above right:
Open Hand, Capitol Complex,
Chandigarh
Photo courtesy: Chandigarh
College of Architecture,
Chandigarh

Martyr's Memorial (not yet fully completed) is located on the edge of the upper level. In the beginning of the Capitol Project, the Punjab Government decided to have a Martyr's memorial which would have the usual tower or wall but Le Corbusier came up with a completely revolutionary idea.

It is situated at the end of the plaza forming an enclosure to the entrance of the Assembly building. The main body of the memorial is ready with the Indian Ashok Chakra and the 'Swastika' like, mythological symbols on the exterior. The symbolic debris inside consisting of components like lion, snake and martyr man already cast in bronze and other elements like the column and broken stone pieces depicting the fall of the foreign rule in India are yet to be executed.

Next in this memorial lies the Open Hand monument which was completed in 1985, a spiritual monument—symbol of peace and silence. Le Corbusier said,

> This emblem has haunted my thoughts for many years to bear witness that harmony is possible among men. Forgetting preparing for war or ceasing cold war.

No architect in the world has thought of raising a spiritual emblem which is not part of his brief, nor could one have the intellect to prepare such a brief. Le Corbusier had to ask for a special approval from the Prime Minister after convincing him of the importance of such a monument.

Le Corbusier Rediscovered

The sculpture symbolizes blessings like those by Buddha—the way our saints used to bless. A symbolic structure with many meanings and connotations, the Open Hand is most startling and significant besides the message it coveys. The overall environment makes the complex sacred and blissful, which empowers one's body and soul.

On the eastern end of the campus is the High Court, last in the series, but first to come up in the complex in 1965. It is a splendid sculpture in the space, ushering in the advent of Modernism in architecture in India, with portals of the portico. The genesis of the form is geometry with barrel vaults, a parasol, double roof like an umbrella to protect the building from the sun and space between two roofs left open to allow free flow of air.

The building has an inspiring and intriguing use of geometry all over, which could be divided in squares and golden sections.

Top:
High Court, Capitol
Complex, Chandigarh
Photo courtesy: Department
of Tourism, Chandigarh

Above left:
Model of the proposed
Governor's Palace
Photo courtesy: Chandigarh
Architecture Museum,
Chandigarh

Above right:
Model of Museum of
knowledge
© FLC-ADAGP

Finally, there is an incomplete edifice i.e. the Governor's Palace. Although planned right in the beginning, Corbusier had been drawing this in his very early study of Chandigarh. The form has several symbolic meanings and connotations; it is a pyramidal mass at the apex location of the city with the backdrop of the Himalayan range—metaphor of Egyptian pyramid, five-storied building at Fatehpur Sikri or Indus Valley ziggurat. The entire building is a symbolic symmetry capped at the top with an inverted curve.

However, this proposal was shelved in 1960 after it was branded undemocratic, which left a gaping void between the Assembly building and the High Court. Le Corbusier was told that such a palace is not given to any government servant in a democratic country, so he designed an alternative which was called the Museum of Knowledge, proposed at the same location.

The Museum of Knowledge was to be a place full of pictures, sounds, electronics, colour graphics, magnetic tape recordings and compact disks. The crux of the museum is a form of dispensing information.

Now the administration is trying to resurrect it to complete the Complex. Once, a decision to use the original design of the Governor's Palace readapted to house functions of a modern-day Museum of Knowledge, after necessary modifications, was taken. Subsequently a lot of work was done under the chairmanship of M.N. Sharma, first Indian chief architect of Chandigarh on the proposal.

However, the complete brief of requirements along with the requirements of space are not yet clear, efforts are being made to formulate the same. And thereafter, lot of work to make modifications in the design of Governor's Palace to be used as a Museum of Knowledge also needs to be done.

In the letter written by Le Corbusier, on 20th December 1960 from Paris, addressed to Dr M.S. Randhawa, Additional Secretary, Government of India, Ministry of Agriculture, he sent the following programme for the building

> My project for 'Museum of Knowledge', at the summit of the Capitol Complex of Chandigarh, can thus be defined.

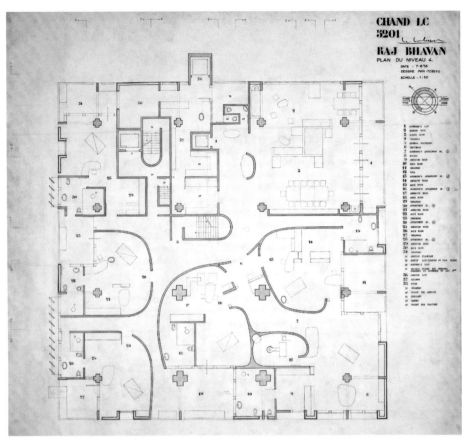

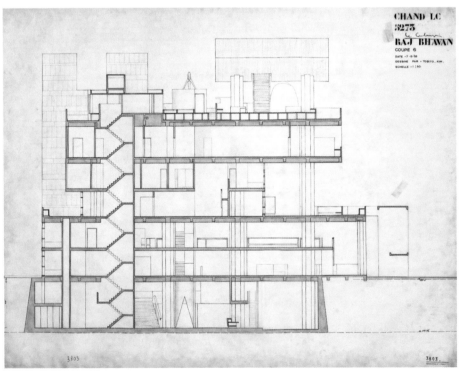

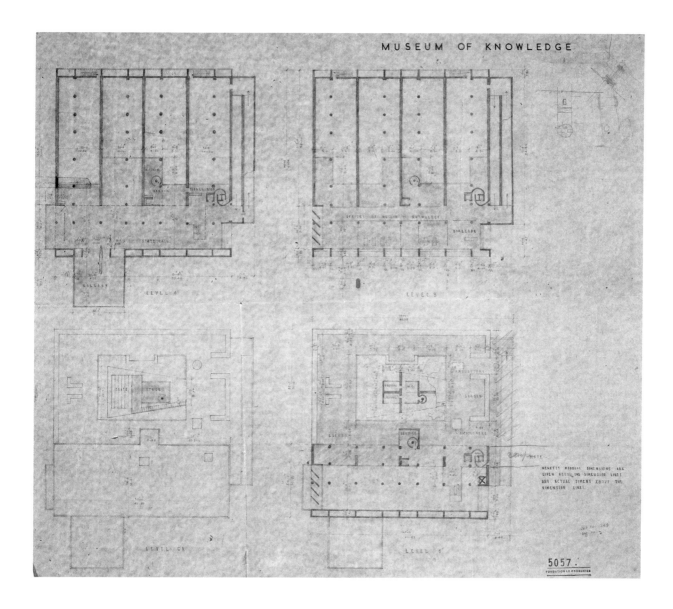

MUSEUM OF KNOWLEDGE

5057.

Proposed plans for Museum
of Knowledge
© FLC-ADAGP

Facing page above:
Plan of the Governor's Palace
© FLC-ADAGP

Facing page below:
Section of the
Governor's Palace
© FLC-ADAGP

'Museum of Knowledge'

The 'round' books will be one of the indirect and complementary
productions of the distinct activities constituting the programmes
of the Palace of Chandigarh.

Four spectator's balconies for projections will occupy one of the
sides of the state rooms opening at will on each of the screens of
the four electronic laboratories which are located in the building
(under the premises reserved for the government) on this screen
will pass the explanations of certain government propositions of the

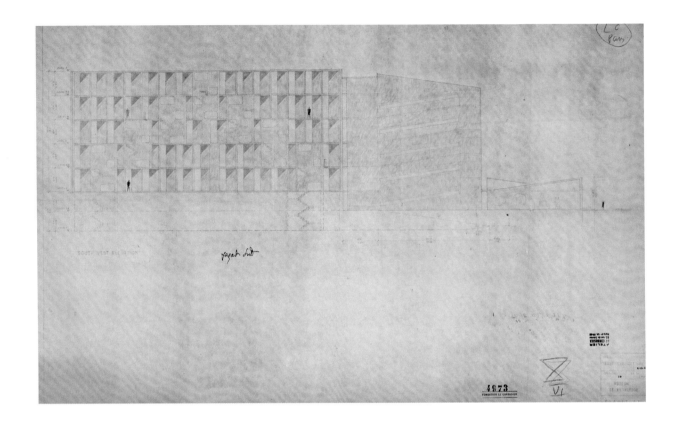

Sketch of proposed elevation
for Museum of knowledge
© FLC-ADAGP

Prime Minister or Chief Minister or the Administrators of the elite of India or even of foreign countries. The four above mentioned laboratories are four empty naves in which continually mobile installations permit the realization of the specific programme of each of the four laboratories.

In this complex, there are several features like pavilion with inverted roof similar to Assembly and Governor's Palace (unbuilt as yet). All the buildings of the complex have the patina of concrete, colour and texture. Le Corbusier had sculpted all the buildings, all express versatility and plasticity and speak of monumental dignity.

Le Corbusier wrote to Mrs Eulie Chowdhury, senior architect on 27th June 1965, from Paris saying that,

> My work in Chandigarh has been completed (in principle). They have been well executed. I refer to the High Court, the Secretariat, the Assembly building, the Governor's house transformed to become, 'Electronic Laboratory of Scientific Decision'.

Well here goes: for many years (fighting against all sorts of countries, with governments, with ministers, with committees of various kinds) I have discovered the necessity for the creation of an electronic laboratory of scientific decision put at the disposal of authority (Prime Minister, chief Minister....) and destined to assure the execution of useful orders concerning the part of the life of a country which is called its urbanism. I attach with this an organic programme which involves the construction of the 'Electronic Laboratory Scientific Decision', which would replace, at the moment, at the summit of the Capitol of Chandigarh, the Governor's house (the Governor having wished and decided to live independently in the town.)

I repeat therefore that the organism that I have provided: 'Electronic Laboratory of Scientific Decision' applies itself very well to the case of a city such as Chandigarh. Will you take this in your hands? Do this because you should not abandon Chandigarh, Capitol of Punjab (your country). Put yourself in contact with Prabhawalker who has all my confidence. I am sending him a copy of this letter.'

In the Capitol Complex, we have the great modern heritage and legacy of Le Corbusier. If his dream gets fulfilled in totality it will give him a lot of solace as the architect who composed this symphony. As it is said that an incomplete statement does not convey the message which the administration is fully aware of and believes in. Certainly, the proposed edifice, in whatever way the decision is taken, will get built and with the contribution of the administration and efforts of Le Corbusier's foundation.

CHANDIGARH: CITY IN GARDEN
Trees as elements of urban design

Rajnish Wattas

Chandigarh is famous for Swiss-French architect Le Corbusier's architectural and planning genius all over the world. Considered as 20th century Modernism's greatest experiment in architecture and urban planning, it was recently inscribed as a UNESCO World Heritage property. However, what is less widely recognised is that it is also perhaps the world's largest experiment in building a capital town inspired by the Garden City movement of the 19th century (popularised by Ebenezer Howard in Britain), significant for its planned green spaces and tree plantations. It is probably the only city on such a large scale—planned for half a million population, now holding nearly 1.2 million people— where landscaping was embedded in its core structure and every tree plantation was planned in detail beforehand. Besides going into the quantitative and qualitative benefits of such extensive scientifically analysed planned green cover, one needs to also examine Chandigarh conceptually, as an aspirational model in attempting to create an urban arcadia for the 20th century 'machine age'. This attempted unique urban paradise (still holding good ground) in the present mostly dismal urban scenario of chaotic and polluted cities of India—if not fiercely protected would eventually also be swamped by the laissez-faire unplanned growth visible in the skylines of Gurgaon, Bengaluru, etc., and many such big Indian cities.

The inception of Chandigarh began with the trauma of partition of the country in 1947 and the urgent need to build a new capital city for the now

truncated state of Punjab apportioned to the Indian side, as well as the pressing need to shelter millions of homeless refugees. Besides the great healing touch that Chandigarh imparted to the traumatised refugees by accommodating them in the new city and giving shelter, its aesthetic landscape perhaps too played a soothing role with its mantle of greenery clothing its built form of brick and concrete.

Before one delves deeper into Chandigarh's landscaping, it is essential to address the question as to what landscape really is? Whenever we experience a building in an urban setting, there is either a foreground or a background comprising some component of vegetation or built-form. So cities are experienced in motion as one continuum of images: both built-up and landscapes. This underscores how critical is the role of nature in cities for a holistic and humane experience of urban areas.

URBAN LANDSCAPING IN INDIA: A HISTORIC PERSPECTIVE

In the Indian tradition knowledge was always transmitted by the guru/ teacher to the disciple beneath a tree as was the occurrence of spiritual

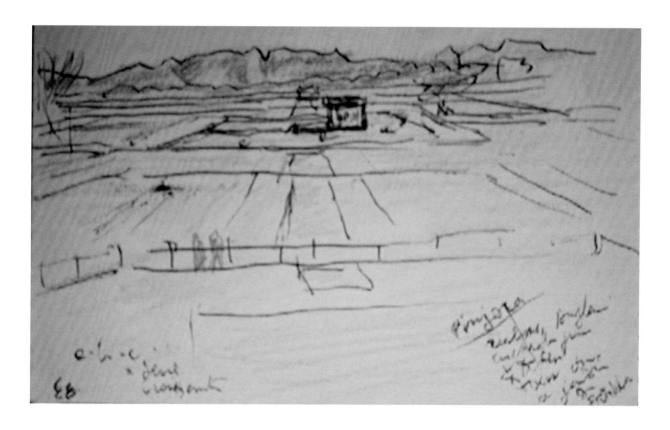

Sketch by Corbusier of Pinjore
Gardens © FLC-ADAGP

enlightenment. Trees were always planted around temples and worshipped, signifying their importance.

In the medieval times in the walled cities of India, because of the fear of invaders, the built-form grain was very dense with winding narrow alleys and self-shading courtyards. The community focal point called *chaupal* usually had some big tree or a grove of shade giving sacred trees like banyans or peepuls where people congregated. As the structures were small and low, people could easily connect with the elements of nature and cosmos with everyday use of roof terraces and courtyards. So there was always a connection with the elements of nature and an experience of surrounding distant landscape, unlike in the present clutter of highrise, densely spaced blocks in the cities mushrooming all over the country.

When the Mughals came they brought to India the great tradition of 'Formal Gardens' that basically originated from the Persian Gardens with their core elements of symmetry, the quadrant *charbagh* and use of water for cooling. Le Corbusier often visited the nearby Mughal Gardens at Pinjore located close to Chandigarh to observe and sketch copiously for possible solutions to deal with the challenge of climatic issues for his proposed buildings.

With the advent of the British Raj in India about 200 years ago, it was decided to use the tools of architecture and landscape to make a political statement of imperial assertion. The grand Central Vista at New Delhi between the Viceroy's Palace (Rashtrapati Bhawan) placed atop the Raisina hill and India Gate is a grandiose, monumental language of landscape. The British civil lines and army cantonments spread all over the country located outside the old, native cities too had Edwin Lutyens' kind of layouts with beautiful, neat tree-lined avenues, gardens and parks.

SEEDS OF CHANDIGARH'S LANDSCAPING

When the Chandigarh project came up, the ruling elites of the post-Independence India steeped in the hierarchal social structure inherited from the British, too wanted to get away from the unhygienic narrow alleys of the old, traditional cities. The old bazaars might have been very picturesque and exotic for the visitors with their aromas and colours, but if one wanted to live there it was not all that romantic for the haves and neo-rich of the country.

When A.L. Fletcher, an important bureaucrat tasked with the preparation of the brief for the new city for the future architect, began his work, there were a lot of uncertainties. Basic questions like a city for how many people, what should be the budget, etc., needed to be addressed What will be the nature of the city: administrative, commercial or mixed? Besides these, there were many other such fundamental issues that needed to be settled and a client's brief created for the future architect-planner of the city. Fletcher, who was widely travelled and familiar with the Garden City movement in Britain was very impressed by the Ebenezer Howard's concept for green towns. Though such experimental towns in Britain were much smaller settlements as an inspirational model for the Chandigarh project, it was nevertheless decided that Chandigarh should have the core attributes of a Garden City. Fletcher wrote a detailed note outlining his stance, which was accepted by the Punjab Government.

Dr M.S. Randhawa, a distinguished senior bureaucrat and a qualified agricultural scientist at that time, too, had an enormous contribution in the landscaping for the city. He exhorted that the new city would urgently require a 'mantle of greenery', as the buildings in the city would come up much faster than the time taken by plantations to take root.

The original team of American architects and planners comprising Albert Mayer and Mathew Nowicki who were initially assigned the Chandigarh project had to be soon replaced by Le Corbusier, owing to the tragic death of Nowicki in a plane crash and Mayer's inability to continue in his

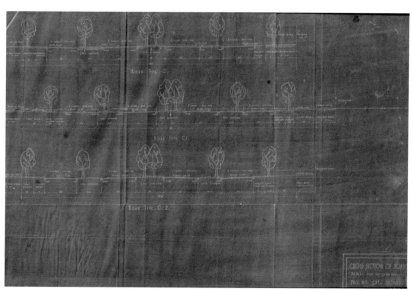

CHANDIGARH

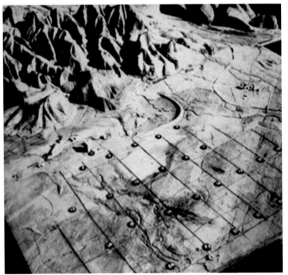

absence. However, the Americans too had shown a strong predilection for weaving in a lot of landscaping components in their conceptual master plan proposed for the city.

Many of the seed ideas underlined by them in this regard, became precursors of what Corbusier too developed later on, including the alignment of the city plan towards the mountains. The other broad similarities of landscape elements between the layout plans developed both by the American and Corbusier teams comprise of a central linear park running throughout the city fabric and of greens running through the heart of each neighbourhood unit. Detailed study of trees suitable for various categories of road sections was also undertaken by them.

CORBUSIER'S ENGAGEMENT WITH LANDSCAPE

During Corbusier's training in an art school in his home town La Chaux-de-Fonds, Switzerland, his brilliant and inspiring teacher Charles L'Eplattenier, made the students go out to the mountains to vigorously sketch pine trees there. They left a great mark on him as he used them as motifs in his early residential projects as kind of modern decoration on their edifices. He was always collecting a repertoire of possible ideas and forms from his observations of nature for future application, and the pine tree became one of those motifs. So his training as a landscape painter influenced him towards establishing a special relationship between landscape and architecture.

He looked at landscape not just as a manicured or patterned garden around him, something that existed only in immediate vicinity. The horizon was very important to him. He always tried to establish a connection between the built-form and the distant views. In Chandigarh it was with the mountains and in Marseille with the sea, so the larger connection mattered a lot to him. And these views were often framed through long continuous ribbon windows as in Villa Savoiye or through a small aperture like in his cabin at Roquebrune-Cap-Martin.

Then we all know of his epic journey *Voyage d'Orient,* and his moment of epiphany at the Acropolis in Athens! For him the Acropolis and the setting of the Parthenon atop the hilltop was intensely inspirational as a brilliant site and structure relationship. This is where he realised the criticality of siting an architectural composition at a vantage point and thereby enhancing its experience for the visitor and making it an element in space both 'visible and yet not so visible'.

And then there is the innovation of creating roof gardens, using the terrace as a tool of establishing a 'man-cosmos' dialogue for the residents of a building. The roof garden is visible in many of his works including Villa Savoye, Villa La Roche, Unité d'habitation and later the Secretariat in the Capitol Complex, Chandigarh.

So at Chandigarh there was a natural connect between the aspirations of the client and the ethos of the architect-planner with the commonality of placing high value on the role of landscape; both at the level of the individual building and the city. The brief for Chandigarh was a 'Garden City-inspired' capital and Corbusier came with a pre-existing special engagement with landscape. The meeting of these two forces shaped the green concept of Chandigarh.

LANDSCAPING GETS UNDERWAY

In the very early stages of work on Chandigarh a Tree Plantation Advisory Committee headed by Dr M.S. Randhawa was formed with Corbusier on board, who undertook systematic documentation, classification of tree species and analysis for their possible use. He made a list of all the major urban spaces requiring tree plantations: roadsides, parks, public squares or special areas like the Sukhna Lake, etc., and analysed possible tree configurations suitable for plantation there. Tree plantation could be in a single row, multiple rows—as heterogeneous or homogeneous rows or in groves. A further analysis of the various horizontal and vertical road sections and the pattern of sun's movement warranting shade, cutting-off glare for comfortable movement of vehicles was undertaken. He wanted to use trees not only for ornamental purposes, but for functional, environmental benefits and for forging interrelationship with the buildings too. In his studies of the movement of the sun he realised that the rising and setting sun in winter, would affect the roads running north-east to south-west axis and glare would get into the eyes of the motorists. He solved this issue by proposing plantation of trees with evergreen spreading canopies that would commingle together at the top, to form protective 'green tunnels'. There is an avenue between Sectors 8 and

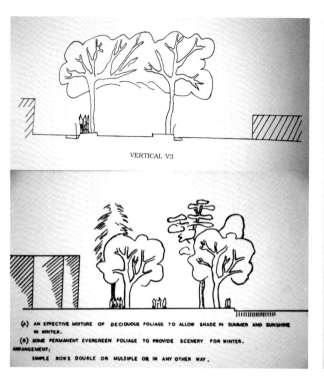

VERTICAL V3

(A) AN EFFECTIVE MIXTURE OF DECIDUOUS FOLIAGE TO ALLOW SHADE IN SUMMER AND SUNSHINE IN WINTER.

(B) SOME PERMANENT EVERGREEN FOLIAGE TO PROVIDE SCENERY FOR WINTER.

ARRANGEMENT:

SIMPLE ROWS DOUBLE OR MULTIPLE OR IN ANY OTHER WAY.

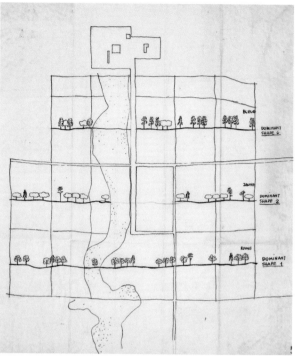

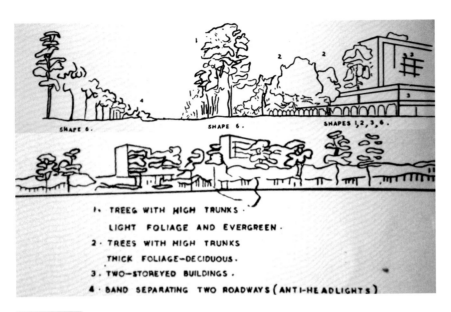

9, running north-east south-west axis, where this can still be seen with beautiful trees on both sides and their foliage commingling with one another to form a veritable 'green tunnel'.

He also looked at the relationship of trees with architecture along major avenues. In a conceptual sketch for the 'Ceremonial Boulevard' Jan Marg, that leads to the Capitol Complex, the first row comprised of small-sized trees, the second row of taller trees and the third row was of the tallest trees, so that a beautiful vista leading the eye to the distant hills and profile of the Assembly and Secretariat buildings was created. Alas, this wonderful composition has now disappeared, and the old species have been replaced by new ones without following the original configuration

Top left:
Le Corbusier's layout plan aligned towards the mountains
Source: Chandigarh Architecture Museum, Chandigarh

Above left:
Tree plantation concept for Chandigarh by Le Corbusier
© FLC-ADAGP

Facing page above:
View of the roundabout on Jan Marg, a V2 avenue
© Rajiv Kumar

Facing page below:
View of Capitol Complex from the Secretariat rooftop
© Rajnish Wattas

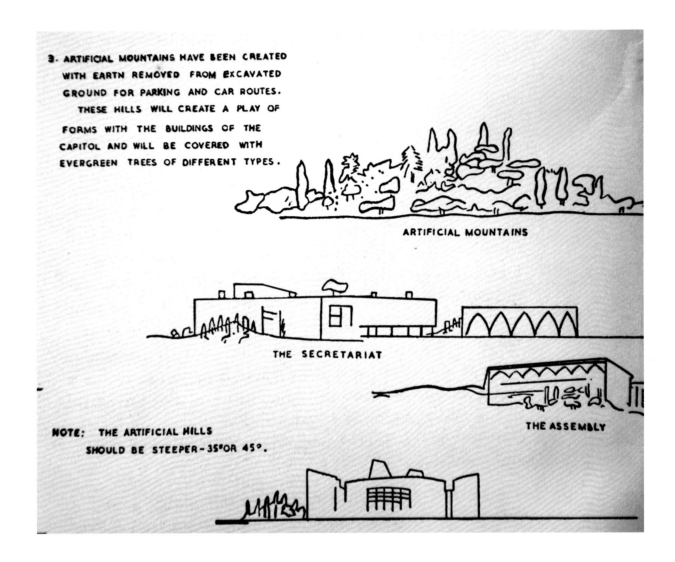

3. ARTIFICIAL MOUNTAINS HAVE BEEN CREATED
WITH EARTH REMOVED FROM EXCAVATED
GROUND FOR PARKING AND CAR ROUTES.
THESE HILLS WILL CREATE A PLAY OF
FORMS WITH THE BUILDINGS OF THE
CAPITOL AND WILL BE COVERED WITH
EVERGREEN TREES OF DIFFERENT TYPES.

ARTIFICIAL MOUNTAINS

THE SECRETARIAT

NOTE: THE ARTIFICIAL HILLS
SHOULD BE STEEPER - 35°OR 45°.

THE ASSEMBLY

and concept. This highlights the gradual dilution of the original, deeply evolved concepts of tree plantations for the city with lacklustre, ad-hoc and piecemeal plantation decisions now.

Regarding the Capitol Complex, the concepts are not very clear as only limited sketches outlining proposed tree plantation ideas exist; though other landscape elements like earthforms and water bodies are more defined and therefore actually executed on site. The tree plantation sketches clearly indicate creation of an artificial hill formed by the earth dug out for building foundations covered by heterogeneous plantation, as a subtle feature to partially conceal the full impact of the Secretariat's huge mass. This is fully developed and can be seen today with that intent. Recently some efforts have been made to clear off some jarring,

Le Corbusier's early sketch indicating heterogeneous plantation on hillock created with dugout earth, at the Capitol Complex
Source: Chandigarh Architecture Museum, Chandigarh

Facing page:
View of the Secretariat rooftop garden
© Rajnish Wattas

wild growth of trees that had come up with the long neglect of the Capitol Complex's landscaping and it has been spruced up now.

Early study sketches by Corbusier for the Secretariat show it as a vertical tower, something like the unbuilt Algiers highrise block designed by him. Later, however, the theme of the unobstructed view of the Himalayas so central to his concepts for the alignment of the city, resonated powerfully enough for him to revise his vertical block proposal for the Secretariat, making it instead a linear horizontal block of nearly 800 feet length. Also P.L. Varma, the then chief engineer of the Capital project, quite clearly told him that India simply did not have the resources and the technology for building a skyscraper. However, in the manner he treated the linear façade of the Secretariat; breaking the monotony of the basic grid with multiple harmonies is akin to the Algiers block facade. He almost brings back the motif of the 'pine tree filigree' back into play— especially visible in the chief minister's block of the Secretariat. So the tree inspired 'ornamentation' motif of his early formative years' projects in his hometown of La Chaux-de-Fonds, keeps appearing again and again in different avatars, and after so many years in Chandigarh all the way!

The other aspect about the Secretariat is the implementation of the 'roof garden' concept of Corbusier, which specially has a double roof to enable growth of plants. When you go to the roof, besides the clusters

Taj Mahal
© Rajnish Wattas

Above left:
Conceptual sketch of 'Governor's Palace' indicating play of landscape elements inspired by Mughal Gardens
© FLC-ADAGP

Trees become 'outdoor
rooms' for street
vendors and hawkers in
Chandigarh's markets and
open spaces
'© Rajnish Wattas

Above right:
Lilac pink blossoms of
Chorisia speciosa tree
along a brick wall
© Rajnish Wattas

of foliage plants and small trees, a notable aspect is the parapet wall all around, thereby blocking immediate view. It is only when you go near the high concrete wall, you realise that while it blocks the immediate view right below the building, it deliberately guides the eye towards the distant horizons. A connection between the plantations of the roof and the distant hills, fields and the bucolic landscape all around is beautifully established.

The sketch for the unbuilt Governor's Palace also indicates a landscape of terraces, water cascades and plantations inspired by Mughal Gardens, connecting it to the main piazza and rest of the edifices.

SALIENT FEATURES OF PRESENT TREE PLANTATION

Notwithstanding the changes/dilution of the original tree plantation concepts in Chandigarh, there are still significant aspects visible today as envisaged in the original planning. Trees, as initially conceived do hold environmental value, functional value, interrelation with architecture and aesthetic value in Chandigarh. Aesthetically, there is a complete cycle of flowering trees like a symphony of colours that keeps changing round the year in the landscape.

One of the key aesthetic concepts regarding trees in the city evolved by Corbusier was that every neighbourhood unit called Sector in the inner continuously running, V4 shopping street would have tree species with a distinct colour of blossoms. A scheme of plantation indicated yellow for Sector 16 shopping street with Cassia fistula trees; pink for Sector 27 with Cassia javanica trees and so on. So the idea was that when people moved along this continuous running V4 road, the distinct colour of blossoms gave identity to each respective Sector through a landscape element.

In the Indian way of life—more than any planner could have ever anticipated—trees provide 'outdoor rooms' for the informal sector of urban services and shelter for the poor migrant populace that the formal city does not cater for. Many street-side hawkers, vendors—the man

Profusely flowering trees define spring in Chandigarh

Facing page above:
Amaltas (*Cassia fistula*)

Facing page below:
Java-ki-rani
(*Cassia javanica*)

Top right:
Jacaranda (*Jacaranda mimosifolia*);

Above right:
Tecoma (*Tecoma argentia*)
© Rajnish Wattas

who fixes punctures on your cycle, the shoeshine boy, the cobbler, tea stall operator and others function under the canopy of the trees in the markets, neighbourhoods or wherever there is a demand for such services. Such low end service providers can't afford shop rentals and so with ingenuity, operate beneath tree canopies. Initially, the city wished them away as encroachers, but soon realised their usefulness to the residents and ratified their activities under a regulated policy.

Now coming to the interrelationship of trees with architecture, we always see a building with a foreground or against a background—it may be of natural settings with trees or in a crowded urban area purely comprise of

built forms, though in Chandigarh it will mostly be the former. One may examine the relationship between the two in terms of scale, form, colour and texture. The height and spread of a tree impacts the perception of scale of a building, and so do contrasting or harmonising colours and textures. Just to cite an example, the *Chorisia speciosa* tree when viewed against the background of brickwork in one instance and when juxtaposed against a concrete façade in another instance, creates varied aesthetic impacts.

In Chandigarh's landscape there is a very beautiful cycle of changing treescapes round the year. The first trees to blossom in early spring are the profusely flowering *Bombax ceibas*. This is followed by another flowering tree *Jacaranda mimosifolia* followed by many more such species with beautiful colours of blossoms, thereby creating a veritable symphony of blossoms on the city skyline. And then there are some trees like *Delonix regia* and *Cassia fistula* that come into a riot of colours, just when summer is at its peak.

There is also a very fascinating phenomenon in the months of March and April, when there is a kind of 'autumn' in spring! There are some non-flowering trees that undergo a huge leaf fall that is followed by sprouting of tender copperish and pale green new leaves. So it's a wonderful landscape and magical, aesthetic experience for city residents.

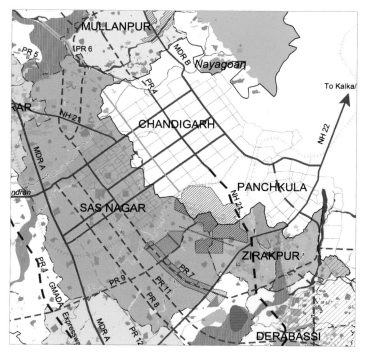

Facing page:
'Autumn in spring' when
deciduous trees like Pilkhan
(*Ficus infectoria*) shed leaves
© Rajnish Wattas.

Above:
Plan indicating satellite towns
adjoining Chandigarh
Photo courtesy: Department of
Urban Planning, Chandigarh

Above right:
High-rise towers coming up in
metropolitan cities
© Rajnish Wattas

CONCERNS

In spite of more than six decades of Chandigarh's inception marked by rapid vibrant growth, the overall fabric is still essentially of a city endowed with rich green open spaces, parks, gardens and exemplary tree cover. It has emerged as the green, oxygenating-lung counter-point to the close by highly polluted and congested national capital of New Delhi. It is also seen in the entire country as a model city known for its holistic living and quality life. At the same time (as elaborated in its Master Plan–2031), the city faces enormous pressures that challenge its future character. So the major concern is how green will the city remain in the coming future? Will it be able to safeguard its 20th century 'Garden City' identity or succumb to the forces of laissez faire urbanisation sweeping across the country or go the way of most big cities, that too were once proudly branded as 'Garden Cities' such as Bengaluru (previously Bangalore) or Edwin Lutyens' colonial New Delhi, but now gasp for clean air and other environmental parameters.

There is an acute shortage of land currently in Chandigarh for any future growth, it being a small 114 sq. km land-locked central government administered pocket, surrounded by adjoining states of Punjab and Haryana. As it is, there is a huge pressure on the city to accommodate the natural growth of its own existing population compounded further by the huge influx of migrants to the city seeking better employment or as a coveted retirement destination. Besides these pressures, the city also has emerged as a major regional hub for commerce, trade and as a gateway to tourism to some neighbouring states. Not surprisingly, the third phase of the city compared to first phase low-rise, plotted development is full of mid-rise apartment blocks. Along with Chandigarh's phenomenal growth the urbanisation pattern of its adjoining satellite towns too has gained a major spurt.

According to the Master Plan projections the city population will grow to 1.8 million people by 2031 from the present 1.2 million. Also the collective population of core city along with that of the adjoining satellite towns called the 'Tricity Urban Complex' will reach 4.5 million by then. All this will radically impact the city character, notwithstanding the safeguards, embedded in the statutory Master Plan–2031.

Presently the Indian Government has placed a huge thrust on creating new 'Smart Cities' across the country besides revamping, sprucing up existing ones and upgrading their infrastructure and services. Can the Garden City inspired Chandigarh be the new role model of development for them to emulate? Not really, as nobody can acquire so much of land as was allotted to Chandigarh in the new urbanisation thrust, for building another low density city. In that case, are vertical green cities the only way forward? Will it be going back to Corbusier's visions of future urbanisation models of vertical cities like The Ville Contemporaine, Plan Voisin and the Cité Radieuse developed from 1922–1939? So these are the questions which need to be addressed.

His various urban theories and the hypothetical models as above mentioned were really a search for the ideal city in the new 'machine age'. Though he was widely criticised for his ideas of 'Vertical Green Cities' then, but actually, when you look at the mushrooming, chaotic high-rise skylines all over the world, and in India too now, you really begin to feel perhaps Corbusier's vision was far ahead of others in thinking of vertical green options for future urbanisation.

In this scenario is Chandigarh well poised to take on the future without losing its green identity? Hopefully.

Facing page:
Modular man at Le Corbusier Centre, Chandigarh
Photo courtesy: Le Corbusier Centre, Chandigarh

ARCHIVING, EXHIBITING AND DISSEMINATING LE CORBUSIER'S LEGACY

A foundation and a modern art collection

Michel Richard

Le Corbusier died on 27 August 1965 at Roquebrune-Cap-Martin, near his Cabanon.

Without direct heirs and driven by the fear that his carefully conserved archives and works would be scattered after his death, Le Corbusier spent the last 15 years of his life conceiving and implementing, down to its smallest details, the project of a Foundation that would bear his name.

> I here declare, for every eventuality, that I leave everything that I possess to an administrative entity, the 'Fondation Le Corbusier', or any other meaningful form, which shall become a spiritual entity, that is, a continuation of the endeavour pursued throughout a lifetime.
>
> To bring together and conserve after his death the writings, paintings, drawings, engravings, tapestries, collections and personal objects that belonged to Le Corbusier.
>
> To place at the disposal of all those who should wish to consult them the records of Le Corbusier's work and research.
>
> Le Corbusier,
> Note dated 13 January 1960.

His most immediate task was to define a legal status, which would ensure both the Foundation's coming into being and its permanence, and provide it with the necessary resources for accomplishing its missions.

On 11 June 1965, Le Corbusier approved the draft statutes of the Foundation which says in its first article:

The institution known as 'Fondation Le Corbusier' has as its aim:

> ▶ to receive, acquire, restore, conserve and make known to the public by all appropriate means (exhibitions, publications, lectures, conferences, films, etc.) the original works, notes, manuscripts, documents, properties and various objects, including those handed over, bequeathed or made over to it by Le Corbusier, or other third parties, being of interest for the

knowledge and the propagation of Le Corbusier's thought and of his plastic, architectural and literary work.

▶ by all appropriate means to encourage architectural research in the sense defined by the written and built work of Le Corbusier.

These statutes have continued up to the present day to govern the running of the Foundation.

On 16 June 1965, the definitive text of Le Corbusier's will confirmed his intention 'of appointing as his sole legatee, the Public Benefit Institution known as Fondation Le Corbusier.'

On 24 July 1968, by a decree of the Council of State, the Foundation was granted recognition as a Public Benefit Institution.

THE FOUNDATION TODAY

The activity of the Foundation currently comprises two main undertakings: preserving the architect's work and collections; circulating his work and spreading his ideas.

Facing page:
Le Corbusier au Cabanon de Roquebrune-Cap-Martin, 1951
Photo: Lucien Hervé
© FLC-ADAGP

Below left and right:
Maison LA Roche-Jeanneret, Paris, 1923-1925
Photo : Cemal Emden, 2015
© FLC-ADAGP

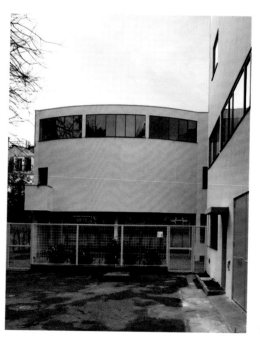

- Defending the author's moral rights. Global monitoring of buildings: conservation, restoration, monitoring, recommendations, etc.

- Preservation and enhancement of works belonging to the Foundation: maintenance of buildings, restoration, organizing visits, publications, etc.

- Maisons La Roche and Jeanneret, the Foundation's head-quarters in the 16th arrondissement in Paris (1925).

- Le Corbusier's studio-apartment, 24 rue Nungesser et Coli in the 16th arrondissement in Paris (1932).

- The Petite Villa on the lake shore at Corseaux (Switzerland) (1924).

Archives and collections

A large part of these is made up of works bequeathed by Le Corbusier to the Foundation and those acquired since his death:

- 35,000 original plans from Le Corbusier's architectural studio
- 40 original or recent models of projects, built or unbuilt (Chandigarh, Marseille, Ronchamp, etc.)
- 6,000 drawings, studies, notebooks, etc.
- 150 lithographs
- 80 paintings by Le Corbusier, Léger, Bauchant, Ghika, etc.
- 40 sculptures in plain or polychrome wood
- 12 tapestries
- 10 enamel plaques
- 400,000 pages of records and documents (correspondence, notebooks, diaries, lectures, manuscripts, mock-ups of books, etc.); various personal items...
- 2,000 books by or about Le Corbusier, including Le Corbusier's personal library
- various audio-visual documents by or about Le Corbusier
- 10,000 photographs of Le Corbusier or of works by him
- furniture and original light fixtures designed by Le Corbusier

Facing page:
Appartement, 24 rue Nungesser et Coli, Boulogne-Billancourt, Atelier.
Peintures: Le Grand Ubu (1949), Taureau IV, Androuet, (1953)
Photo: Willy Rizzo
Source: FLC-ADAGP

Diffusing knowledge of Le Corbusier's work in all its aspects (architectural and sculptural work, theoretical work, etc.), including:

- organizing visits of the buildings belonging to the Fondation and promoting visits in all buildings open to visitors;
- receiving researchers, curators, iconographers in the Foundation's premises at Square du Docteur Blanche in the 16th arrondissement in Paris;
- awarding scholarships to young researchers and artists;
- organizing exhibitions and lending works to institutions for exhibitions;
- producing publications;
- organizing meetings, seminars, etc.

LOANS OF WORKS FOR EXHIBITIONS

Much of the Foundation's activity involves responding to requests from the organizers of exhibitions on Le Corbusier or on artistic trends of

Villa Le Lac, Corseaux, 1923
Photo: Olivier Martin-Gambier 2006
© FLC-ADAGP

Facing page from
top clockwise:
La Cheminée, Huile sur toile, 1918, FLC 134

La mer, sculpture bois naturel et polychrome, 1964, FLC 36

Haute Cour, Chandigarh, 1952, encre de Chine sur calque épais, FLC 4574

Millowner's Association Building, (ATMA), Ahmedabad, 1954, Photo : FLC, 2008
© FLC-ADAGP

his time, through loans of works, objects and documents belonging to the collections.

- 2005: Prato, Strasbourg, Sao Paulo, Brasilia, Recife
- 2006: Geneve, Madrid, Grenade, Nantes, Nancy, Cuba
- 2007: Tokyo, Rotterdam, Chandigarh
- 2008: Lisbonne, Liverpool, Ahmedabad, Hiroshima, Yokkaishi
- 2009: Rio de Janeiro, Brasilia, NBelo Horizonte, Ahmedabad, Londres, Berlin, Tokyo, Buenos Aires, Izmir
- 2010: Curitiba, Madrid
- 2011: Las Palmas, Besançon
- 2012: Moscou, Sao paulo, Rome, Munich, La Chaux-de-Fonds
- 2013: Stockholm, Bruxelles, New York, Marseille, Tokyo, Montréal
- 2014: Barcelone, Madrid

In 2015, due to the commemoration of the 50th anniversary of Le Corbusier's death, three important exhibitions have been organized in France: Centre

Nu féminin lisant, crayon
graphite, encre de couleur sur
papier, FLC 3399
© FLC-ADAGP

Pompidou ('Le Corbusier—The Measures of man'), Cité de l'Architecture et du Patrimoine ('Chandigarh – fifty years after Le Corbusier'), and a show dedicated to 'L'oeuvre dessiné' at Musée Picasso, Antibes (then in 2016 at Musée Picasso, Münster, Germany). Exhibitions are also organized in different countries (Hong Kong, Shenzen, Tokyo, etc.), a special exhibition on Le Corbusier's photography organized by the Swiss Embassy in India has been presented in Chandigarh and has been held in five other places (Ahmedabad, Delhi, etc.).

PUBLICATIONS

The Foundation ensures that books published in Le Corbusier's lifetime—in particular works belonging to the collection *L'Esprit Nouveau (Vers une architecture, Urbanisme, L'Art décoratif aujourd'hui, Précisions*, etc.) or titles that are essential for knowledge of his work: *l'Oeuvre complète* in eight volumes published by Willi Boesiger and Hans Girsberger, *La Petite Maison, Le Poème de l'Angle droit*, etc.—are available in French. It equally encourages publication in foreign languages.

The Foundation has also launched an operation to publish Le Corbusier's written work, texts as yet unpublished or that have not so far been published systematically: lectures, correspondence and articles in reviews.

The Foundation supports a great number of academic or general publications facilitating access to documentation and iconography and by granting reproduction rights to publishers.

MEETINGS/SYMPOSIUMS

Nearly every year the Foundation organizes 'Rencontres', open to all those interested in developing their knowledge of Le Corbusier's work. Lectures are given by specialists. These events are also an opportunity to meet surviving eyewitnesses of the architect's work. They give rise to publications issued by the Foundation.

In 2011 the Rencontres were devoted to the anniversary of the Travel to the East and were organized in Istanbul, Athens and Naples.

In 2012, they were devoted to the relation of Le Corbusier with photography.

Considering the importance of this matter for the Foundation, the Foundation decided to organise in 2015 a conference on conservation and restoration of Le Corbusier's built work in Paris at the Institut national d'histoire de l'art.

FURNITURE ISSUES AND HOUSE FITTINGS

Since 1965, the Foundation and beneficiaries of the co-authors have entrusted furniture issues to the firm of Cassina Spa, sole licensee for Le Corbusier models and those produced in collaboration with Pierre Jeanneret et Charlotte Perriand.

The Foundation endeavours to issue models designed by Le Corbusier but which have remained un-issued, or to reissue models no longer available.

Light fixtures designed by Le Corbusier are now reissued with the Italian firm Nemo.

Below left:
L'invention d'un architecte. Le voyage en Orient de Le Corbusier. XVIIe Rencontres de la Fondation Le Corbusier, Istanbul, Athènes, Naples, 2011
© FLC-ADAGP

Below:
L'atelier de la recherche patiente, Éditions Vincent, Fréal et Cie, Paris, 1960
© FLC-ADAGP

Conservation of Le Corbusier's Architectural Work

CONSERVE/RESTORE

As the legatee and direct offshoot of its creator Le Corbusier, the Foundation holds the moral rights to this work and therefore has a duty to constantly watch over his architectural work (and indeed the artist's entire legacy).

We do not plan to treat Le Corbusier's constructions as museums. Rather, we wish to bring to light their living character; that is to say, in conserving their original uses as much as possible, we can best guarantee their permanence.

It must first be emphasized that before tackling archaeological, technical and ethical issues, which are of course at the heart of its concerns, the Foundation must overcome a number of obstacles

LOCATION AND COMPLEXITY OF THE ARCHITECTURAL WORK

Relatively modest in quantitative terms, Le Corbusier's architectural work has the following characteristics:

- ▶ it is spatially extensive, distributed across eleven countries on four continents. If the majority of works are in Europe, in particular France and Switzerland, some buildings—and by no means the least important—are located in the states of the Chandigarh (a Union Territory) and Gujarat in India, and others in Tunisia, Japan, Iraq, Argentina and the USA;

- ▶ these buildings are very different in nature and in size: they include villas and houses, cultural buildings, multi-family housing, office buildings, gymnasiums, stadiums, etc.;

- ▶ their conservation status also varies greatly;

- ▶ as is well known, legislation or heritage protection policy may differ greatly from one country to another.

Loge du jardinier,
Villa Savoye, Poissy,
Restauration 2015
Photo: FLC, 2015
© FLC-ADAGP

Facing page:
La Cité de Refuge de
Le Corbusier: restauration
Photo: Olivier Martin-
Gambier, 2015
© FLC-ADAGP

We live today in a transitional period that knows a double phenomenon: an important transformation in regards to proprietors and/or uses; and the awareness of the high quality of these works, accompanied by a desire to bring to light their original spirit. This evolution entails some very positive consequences, but it also conceals a certain number of threats:

▶ With the natural passing of generations, the individual houses change or will change owners.

▶ Other buildings will be required to adapt, whether to new uses or new norms—hygiene, security, environmental criteria, etc. Otherwise, they will be required to take into account new constraints, such as tourist visits, that risk to alter the quality of authenticity or originality that contributed to their notoriety. The city of Chandigarh in particular comes to mind: confronted with demographic growth, it should respond to new demands in terms of housing, public transport, etc.

Each of his buildings constitute a piece of art in and of itself. Each issue concerned in the restoration of Le Corbusier's buildings is effectively governed by this specificity. As we face today a set of rules dictating the world of construction—and these rules grow more and more strict— we find that it's a matter of respecting, down to the slightest detail, the original spirit of the work without betraying or weakening it, of retracing the 'out of bounds' attitude that first inspired its edification.

INFORM / DIALOGUE / EXCHANGE / NETWORK

The Foundation has developed an arrangement providing it at all times with the most reliable information possible on the current state of buildings and the likelihood of possible changes. This arrangement involves a network of the buildings' owners, with which the Foundation is in regular contact. It also has an unsolicited network of correspondents in all the countries concerned, informing it without fail of suspicious movements or serious threats.

In most countries, the Foundation is in constant contact with State services and is systematically concerned in the review and monitoring of projects for which they are responsible. This does not necessarily mean that there is always a consensus of opinions on projects under review, but it is an instance of productive discussion.

CONSERVE / DOCUMENT / DIFFUSE

For the Foundation, each building is a work of art, a prototype, a unique experience, a clue to Le Corbusier's creative process. Furthermore, it constitutes an important step in the chronology of various restoration campaigns.

Any renovation, restoration project, or accident, even, grants us the opportunity to enrich our material knowledge of a work, to understand its evolution, its building process, the hazards of its construction... For this reason, it is critical that the Foundation be involved in the studies and the work accomplished during restoration. Research undertaken,

Facing page:
*L'œuvre architecturale
de Le Corbusier. Une
contribution exceptionnelle
au Mouvement Moderne*
© FLC-ADAGP

updated materials, and discovered documents enhance the history and comprehension of the edifice. The analysis of these living archives in light of the documents conserved by the Foundation offers the opportunity to benefit from a fruitful interface. Such archives nourish scientific research and stimulate interest in the restoration of the building in question. For these reasons, the conservation of current and future archives has become a question of the utmost importance for architects and proprietors: it prevents them from wasting precious time, it allows them to confirm their hypotheses, and even permits them to avoid significant errors.

▶ All restoration and development projects, including for executing architectural projects by Le Corbusier, are submitted to an international committee of experts. Its role is both to contribute to the need to respect Le Corbusier's original work and to make recommendations on the basis of which the Foundation's Governing Board can either authorize applications addressed to it or express its reservations.

▶ This expertise involves experts being sent regularly to advise owners, allocatees or occupants of buildings executed by Le Corbusier before and during the restoration process.

▶ The monitoring of restoration projects is carried out by the Foundation architect, who also has the role of consultant to the owners. In this capacity, she contributes to research undertaken in the Foundation's archives, she organises the network of owners and contractors and coordinates the Foundation's initiatives with the territorial authorities and state territorial authorities.

▶ She ensures that archives of architectural restoration work are put together as the work progresses, by collecting the research undertaken for each restoration project: historical study, technique, planning application file, monochrome samplings, etc. and where possible, retrieving authentic components removed during restoration work. All these elements will ultimately enable more detailed knowledge of each of the buildings created by Le Corbusier and consequently facilitate maintenance on the long term. They also contribute to improve overall knowledge of the work's gestation and meaning.

APPLICATION OF LE CORBUSIER'S ARCHITECTURAL WORK FOR INSCRIPTION ON THE UNESCO WORLD HERITAGE LIST

Besides being responsible for keeping alive Le Corbusier's knowledge and spirit, and gathering precious archives consulted on a daily basis by researchers worldwide, the Foundation is carrying out a most important task to preserve his architectural work, by its participation to the proposed inclusion of the work of Le Corbusier as an outstanding contribution to the Modern Movement in the UNESCO World heritage List.

Seven countries have joined forces in this undertaking: Argentina, Belgium, Germany, India, Japan, Switzerland and France. Seventeen major works are involved. The aim of this transnational serial nomination is to fight for recognition of the buildings and sites constructed by Le Corbusier worldwide as exceptional and as milestones of the Modern Movement that influenced the practice of architecture everywhere. The application was submitted in January 2015, and the evaluation of the site was carried out by ICOMOS experts in October 2015. The decision of the World Heritage committee was announced in August 2016 and Le Corbusier's work as an outstanding contribution to the Modern Movement was finally included in the UNESCO World Heritage List.

———————

CHANDIGARH
GARDEN CITY TO SMART CITY

AVANT LE SMART LE CORBUSIER
Reinventing Chandigarh in the age of Smart Cities

Jagan Shah

The UNESCO World Heritage Centre has listed Chandigarh's Capitol in a serial listing of 'world heritage' works by Charles Edouard Jeanneret—the irrepressible genius of 20th century architecture and urbanism who practiced under the title 'Le Corbusier'. While the recognition is really about the architectural genius displayed in the sculptural facades with windows sheltered by sunshades, swooping rooflines, and monumental spaces cast in *beton brut*, the setting of this architecture within an urban landscape also designed by Corbusier is a rare combination. And made rarer still by the fact that Chandigarh is being developed into a Smart City under the Government of India's Smart City Mission. This happy circumstance can unfold a new engagement with what Chandigarh is and what it represents; and how the Smart City of Chandigarh can become a new model for a fast-urbanising India that is in search of models for sustainable urbanism.

The modernity of Chandigarh city is easy to witness. The perfectly created streets intersecting at right angles and roundabouts, the street design with green strips and service lanes, the strictly regulated architecture of the government housing, the lush greenery and the Lake, and the iconic buildings of the Capitol Complex, the Secretariat, the High Court and the Assembly—all these combine to make this the first new capital of democratic India. Jawaharlal Nehru had declared: 'Let this be a new town symbolic of the freedom of India, unfettered by the traditions of the past, an expression of the nation's faith in the future.' Corbusier found inspiration in such grand visions. His competition entry for the Palace of the League of Nations in Geneva (1927) and the design for the Palace of the Soviets in Moscow (1928-31) are powerful statements of political vision. The interpretation of grandiose statements is always a comfortable envelope for the architect, as it gives him the latitude of interpretation. With a stridency unparalleled in the 20th century, Le Corbusier called for 'universal...Total city planning,' urging the statesmen and architects of his era: 'let's make our plans... on a scale with twentieth-century events... Huge!' As we will argue later, his public works were conceived for the public; the modern citizen was to be its greatest beneficiary.

With typically Modernist heroism, Corbusier proclaimed that cities could be anywhere: free of context, history or tradition. His infamous proposal of 1925 to raze the centre of Paris and build skyscrapers instead was an early indication of this misplaced heroism. In fact, his early oeuvre is marked by the enthusiasm characteristic of the Art Nouveau and its fascination with the new millennium; which ironically turned out ugly soon after, with the onset of the First World War. By the time Corbusier landed in India, the world had changed from those early days, which rode on the 19th century wave that created Soviet Russia and two ghastly world wars, to the post Second World War era of new nation-states, a superpower America, and rising ambitions in the global South.

SMART ARCHETYPES FOR MODERN TOWN PLANNING

Chandigarh was the first exercise in new city planning that defined the Indian government's approach to urban development for six decades following decolonisation: the development of new tracts of land into fully-serviced habitations that expanded the lifestyles which were lived and defined mainly by the employees of the growing nation-state and their dependents. The culture of India's cities and their economic processes were profoundly altered by the growth of the government and its numerous establishments, which all followed a standardised, almost military planning logic. This was a period during which India made a bold attempt to break with her past through a socio-urban experiment that included, along with an innovative master plan, Modernist buildings, new land-use patterns, provisions for education, recreation, medical and

Facing page:
About: Existing land use map of Chandigarh
Source: Smart City Proposal Annexure 3; Chandigarh Municipal Corporation, Aecom & PwC, 2016 (page no. 8)

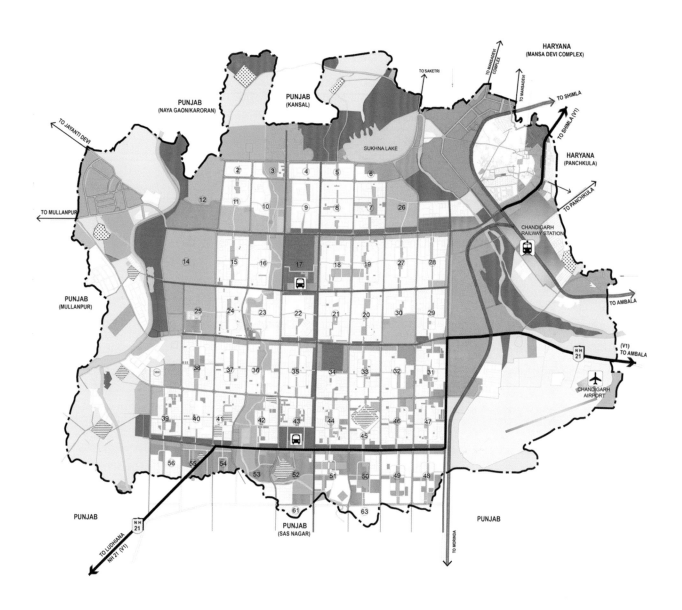

HARYANA
(MANSA DEVI COMPLEX)

PUNJAB
(NAYA GAON/KARORAN)

PUNJAB
(KANSAL)

TO SAKETRI

TO MANSADEVI COMPLEX

TO MANSADEVI

TO SHIMLA

TO SHIMLA (V1)

HARYANA
(PANCHKULA)

TO JAYANTI DEVI

SUKHNA LAKE

TO PANCHKULA

TO MULLANPUR

CHANDIGARH
RAILWAY STATION

TO AMBALA

PUNJAB
(MULLANPUR)

NH 21

(V1)
TO AMBALA

CHANDIGARH
AIRPORT

PUNJAB

NH 21

TO LUDHIANA
NH 21 (V1)

TO MORINDA

PUNJAB

PUNJAB
(SAS NAGAR)

legend

TRANSPORTATION

- MAJOR ROADS
- INTERNAL ROADS
- MAJOR JUNCTIONS / CHOWKS
- RAILWAY STATION
- RAILWAY LINE
- BUS TERMINAL
- CITY BUS NETWORK
- MAJOR BUS STOPS

OPEN SPACES AND WATER FEATURES

- PUBLIC OPEN SPACES / PARKS
- AGRICULTURE
- PLANT, FRUIT NURSERY AND ORCHARDS
- FOREST
- RIVERS, CANALS, LAKE AND WATER BODIES / PONDS

LANDUSE

- RESIDENTIAL
- URBAN VILLAGES
- PERIPHERAL VILLAGES
- COMMERCIAL
- INDUSTRIAL
- EDUCATIONAL INSTITUTES
- HOSPITAL AND HEALTH INSTITUTIONS

- I.T. PARK
- INSTITUTIONAL / OFFICES
- CULTURAL
- VACANT LAND
- OTHERS
- SERVICES & INFRASTRUCTURE

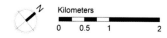

Kilometers

0   0.5   1   2

social services, the careful and deliberate inclusion of ideas that had their origin in a culture far removed from her own.

Corbusier had already in 1931 drafted the Athens Charter along with a group of other Modernists of the CIAM (International Congresses of Modern Architecture), which echoed his obsession with the plan. He famously proclaimed: 'The Plan is the Generator.' Like an immersive classroom, Chandigarh demonstrates that the plan is indeed the generator. Not unlike the cities of the Indus Valley civilisation or the Roman phalanx, the fabric of streets, open spaces and buildings is ordered for functional efficiency and easy replication: an administrative logic that can only be implemented in a new city.

The insistence on order was emblematic of modern town planning. The street grid represents the archetypal standardisation, composed of an urban block that can be repeated multiple times to create the total urban form. The sector module of 800x1200 metres in Chandigarh creates neighbourhood units for a population ranging between 5,000 to 20,000 inhabitants. Each sector was imagined as a low density, green and functional model, well-equipped with its own maintenance organisations, access to provisions, schools, and domestic services. The boundary of each neighbourhood was contained in a unit marked by V3's, and the street hierarchy ensured that no door from a residence was to open on to a main road. The Sector becomes a permeable, intimate, self-contained unit, traversed on foot or bicycle, on pathways protected by a dense seasonal tree cover. Within each Sector were winding streets where all the public facilities were placed, along the green belts. Naturally, this kind of order was meant to engender the new lifestyle of a secular, orderly and industrious society. And as an administrative capital, the city does justice to its users, giving them 'sun, space and verdure' to live a healthy and productive life.

It is not surprising that in Chandigarh's entry for the Smart City Challenge, the Municipal Corporation of Chandigarh has mentioned the city's planning as the most significant 'opportunity':

> Uniform planning allows ease of implementation – Uniformity of planning and the Sectors ensures replicability of ABD [area-based development] solutions in other parts of the city and makes implementation of smart solutions easy and practical.

Indeed, the replicable planning of the Smart City proposal for Chandigarh can result in a complete rejuvenation of the city, which enjoys the efficiency of modern planning in one respect while it suffers the failures of modern planning on the other, thus needing smart solutions.

The proposal lists the next important opportunity as its 'Heritage status,' which 'will boost the domestic and international tourism.' For the first time since it was built, the city's economic driver has been changed from an administrative and residential centre to a centre for tourism. This also alters the relationship that the bulk of users have with the city. From a city that is famous for being a playground for its indigenous population, it now needs to service and entertain and do business with a larger floating population of tourists, increasing footfalls in public spaces that have been largely devoid of people. With the growth in the services industry, which will preponderate as the source of new jobs, there will be newer professionals looking for places to stay in the city. While it might be debated on the armchairs of India whether it is smart for a city to be friendly to newcomers, the evidence from cities in India and the world is that the urban economy flourishes from the innovation that is generated by cosmopolitan populations.

With the UNESCO nomination comes the need for a heritage management plan, which will influence the planning and management of infrastructure. Chandigarh will need to become a place to visit because of its architectural significance as well as a vibrant economy and culture. The achievement of the primary 'Smart' goal—better quality of life—is intertwined with the achievement of a smarter social order:

> With high level of social inclusion, diversity and gender equality in jobs, 98.51% Aadhar coverage, financial inclusion with 100 % population opening accounts under Jan Dhan Yojna, the city has opportunity to provide equal opportunity for all including framing of effective social security Direct-benefit transfer schemes.

Chandigarh can be a leading example of a Smart City in India which has its roots in a somewhat distant Greenfield city in post-Independence India, and now one of the leading cities in the country, with a high human development index and a per capita income of INR 156,961 (2013-14) which is the 3rd highest in the country. It is this curious

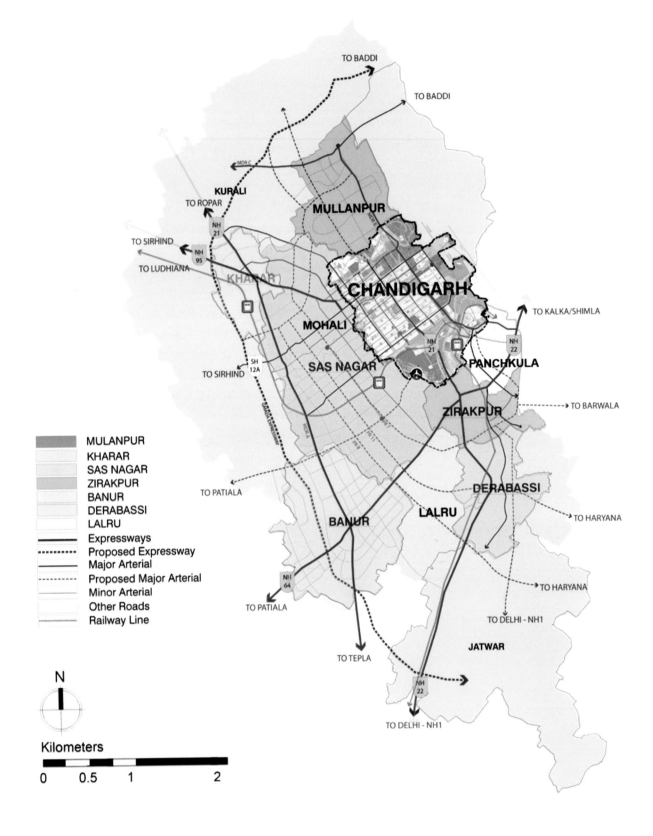

TO BADDI

TO BADDI

MDR-C

KURALI

TO ROPAR

NH 21

TO SIRHIND

NH 95

TO LUDHIANA

KHARAR

MULLANPUR

CHANDIGARH

MOHALI

TO KALKA/SHIMLA

NH 21

NH 22

PANCHKULA

SAS NAGAR

SH 12A

TO SIRHIND

TO BARWALA

ZIRAKPUR

MULANPUR
KHARAR
SAS NAGAR
ZIRAKPUR
BANUR
DERABASSI
LALRU

Expressways
Proposed Expressway
Major Arterial
Proposed Major Arterial
Minor Arterial
Other Roads
Railway Line

TO PATIALA

DERABASSI

TO HARYANA

LALRU

BANUR

TO HARYANA

NH 64

TO DELHI - NH1

TO PATIALA

TO TEPLA

JATWAR

N

Kilometers

0   0.5   1   2

NH 22

TO DELHI - NH1

combination of a growth story, the demand for Chandigarh as a place of economic activity, and its Modern Heritage, comprising both the modern architecture and planning, the built reality, as well as the social experiment of organised collective living, which makes Chandigarh Smart City such a compelling proposition.

But the changing tides of history do not take long to touch the city's shores, even if it is built on 'virgin', 'green-field' territory. The proposal submitted by Chandigarh counts as its primary 'Threats' the city's location within a region in which smaller dispersed townships in Punjab and Haryana burden its infrastructure with through traffic movement every day. Furthermore, the neighbouring cities of Mohali and Panchkula, which have available 'larger land parcels' are able 'to attract investment, finance and service industry as well as Knowledge institutions.'

The 'real threat' stated by the Municipal Corporation is the 'outward migration of productive human resource.' If human resources have to be conserved and attracted, Chandigarh needs to attract younger workers, and those workers will need new occupations, new enterprises and new types of trade and commerce. Given that the bulk of the new jobs will be created in the services and SME (Small and Medium Enterprises) sectors, Chandigarh has to make space for this new generation of residents who will contribute to its future. However, it will have to resolve to accommodate more population. The tantalising possibility in Chandigarh is because it has been protected from density; however, the time has come that it must welcome density without creating congestion. Certainly, Corbusier was not averse to multi-storeyed housing. Smart City Chandigarh is investing large sums of public funds into smart urban infrastructure. Allowing larger numbers of people to use this infrastructure on a daily basis, without letting Chandigarh get swallowed by its region will require higher amounts of public revenue. The benefits of agglomeration in a denser, more vibrant Chandigarh are likely to result in economic benefits.

NO 'CLEAN SLATE'; ONLY PALIMPSEST

By exploring the realm of ideas from where Corbusier's urbanism originates, we discover a vast heritage, which is tangible in the forms of literature, buildings and this singular city, and intangible in the permeation of thought that informs all modern town planning. The evolution of

Corbusier's works is intertwined with the evolution of urbanism and the growth of cities worldwide during the Post-World War II era. Corbusier received a front-seat view of the two powerful poles of modern India, the industries and their leaders, in cities like Ahmedabad and Mumbai, and the political and executive wings of government, in Chandigarh. Wherever Corbusier travelled during his times: from Soviet Russia to Argentina, from New York to Tokyo, from North Africa to India, he carried the spirit of the Modernist *avant garde*, the tenacity of a salesman, the precision of a watch engraver and the hope of a tragic poet. Not everyone understood him well; and he didn't quite understand everyone; thus the tragic end that he chose for himself.

In the mythologies surrounding Chandigarh, there is this image of Le Corbusier surveying the site of the new political capital for Punjab, conceived after the Partition as a way to assuage the loss of Lahore, the historical capital of Punjab, from the window of an airplane. This is the kind of vantage point that was already felt necessary for the city planner; a perspective which allowed the planner to 'see' that which s/he later captures in drawings. In this respect, Chandigarh is the archetypal 'green field' city. It assumed that the land is unencumbered, and created the conditions for that by acquiring land from farmers. Not surprisingly, there were protests from villagers when their lands were being acquired to create the new city. Eventually the land was acquired. Le Corbusier did not have to witness the protests as these were in fact seen by his predecessor, the American urban planner Albert Mayer, part of the first team of American experts that worked on the new capital, who recorded these in routine field notes he sent back to his New York headquarters. It was Mayer that created the green field site for Corbusier.

The early phase of Corbusier's work displayed a streak of creative genius at a time when tastes and lifestyles were being redefined. India got to see a later Corbusier, getting weary of travelling the world to sell the 'radiant city' (La Ville Radieuse, 1934) but also experimenting with other ideas like the linear city of Arturo Soria e Mata and Edgar Chambless's visionary 'road town' (1910) – and then, suddenly, being called on to deliver a new city by the Indian government.

Just as his early skyscrapers showcased the innovations made by the architects of Chicago, taken to a monumental scale, Corbusier's urbanism

Facing page:
About: Chandigarh's vision within the Smart City Proposal
Source: Smart City Proposal Annexure 3; Chandigarh Municipal Corporation, Aecom & PwC, 2016 (page no. 12)

CITIZEN ENGAGEMENT

Public Transportation
Traffic Congestion
Cycle tracks   Dormitories for students
Affordable Housing   **Jobs**
Safety on Streets
Digitization & E-services
Inadequate Parking
Dead Spaces

SWOT ANALYSIS

High HDI   Inadequate Public Transport
Major Regional Center   High Private
among 5 most livable cities in India **Vehicle Ownership**
Regional Knowledge Hub   Untapped tourism potential
Unesco Heritage Status Traffic Congestion & Pollution
98.5 % Adhaar coverage   Increase in lifestyle diseases
Strong Sports infrastructure   Outward Migration
Model Solar city   Overburdened Infrastructure

CITY PROFILE

Strategic Location
Planned Heritage
Green Infrastructure   High Vehicle density
3rd Highest Per-Capita Income **Out Migration**
97.3% Urban population
High Literacy Rate
100% coverage of sewerage system
38% area under green cover

CHANDIGARH **vision**

A Vibrant and Unique Regional Centre, the City Beautiful is envisioned to become a leader in Livability, Sustainability, Equality and Innovation.

was also informed by the global legacy of innovations in town planning, especially the Garden city invented by Sir Ebenezer Howard. Garden cities were intended to be planned, self-contained communities surrounded by 'greenbelts', containing proportionate areas of residences, industry, and agriculture; moving away from the congested industrial town to healthy urban settlements.

The origins of Chandigarh are visible also in Corbusier's idea of the Radiant City (1933), a city of open public space, where buildings were raised above the ground on pilotis (pillars) and the landscape flowed uninterruptedly throughout the city. In Chandigarh, Corbusier created a striated sequence of built and open spaces, the green strips forming parks, play grounds and other recreational zones at the neighbourhood level, extending lengthwise through each sector to enable every resident to lift their eyes to the changing panorama of Himalayas.

Among the ideas that inform Chandigarh, in which we must include his prototype for modern housing, the Domino house, the most significant for Smart City development is 'Les Sept Voies de Circulation', or Seven Vs (via, or roads). As explained on the website of the Chandigarh Administration, the 7Vs establishes a hierarchy of traffic circulation: arterial roads (V1), major boulevards (V2) Sector definers (V3), shopping streets (V4), neighbourhood streets (V5), access lanes (V6) and pedestrian paths and cycle tracks (V7s and V8s). 'The essence of his plan for Chandigarh rests on preserving intact the true functions of these seven types of roads.'

THE (SMART) PLAN IS THE GENERATOR

While the Smart City mission follows the discourse of 'new urbanism', the concept is actually a repudiation of Corbusier and other Modernists of his generation. Chandigarh offers us an opportunity for 'place-making', which is unparalleled by any other city in India, and this opportunity is visible only when we consider the public nature of cities. It is the public-ness of Chandigarh—the Seven Vs creating a labyrinth of public spaces throughout the city, culminating in plazas in the commercial, educational and administrative centres, which is the true asset of the city. By taking the matrix of the Seven Vs and the open spaces, the city can create a public realm of astounding magnitude and beauty. And the infrastructure

Facing page:
Area selected for improvement under the Area Based Development within the Smart City Proposal
Source: Smart City Proposal Annexure 3; Chandigarh Municipal Corporation, Aecom & PwC, 2016 (page no. 13)

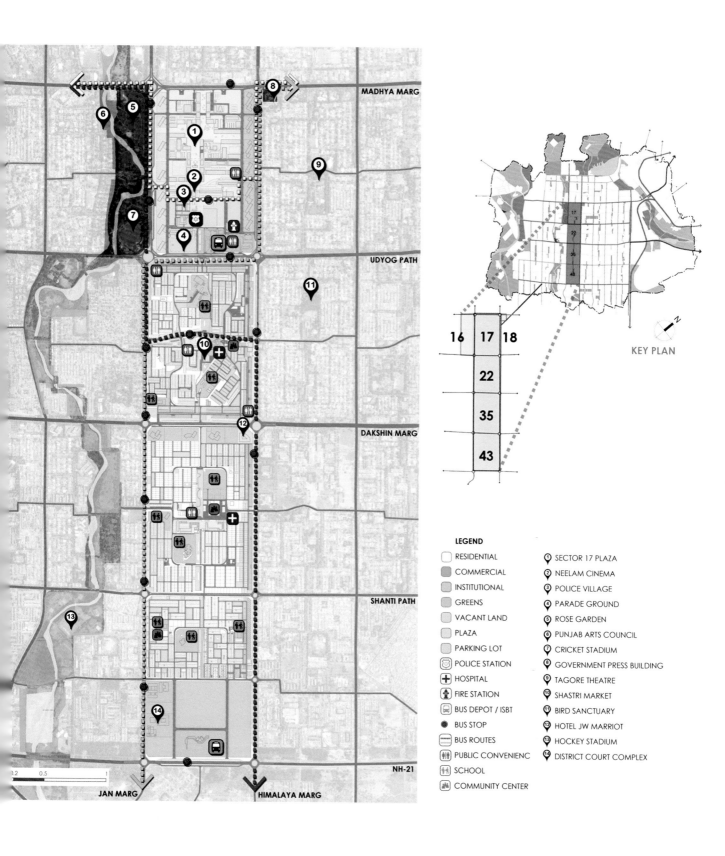

MADHYA MARG

UDYOG PATH

DAKSHIN MARG

SHANTI PATH

JAN MARG   HIMALAYA MARG   NH-21

KEY PLAN

16 17 18
22
35
43

LEGEND

☐ RESIDENTIAL
☐ COMMERCIAL
☐ INSTITUTIONAL
☐ GREENS
☐ VACANT LAND
☐ PLAZA
☐ PARKING LOT
☐ POLICE STATION
✚ HOSPITAL
☐ FIRE STATION
☐ BUS DEPOT / ISBT
● BUS STOP
┉ BUS ROUTES
☐ PUBLIC CONVENIENC
☐ SCHOOL
☐ COMMUNITY CENTER

① SECTOR 17 PLAZA
② NEELAM CINEMA
③ POLICE VILLAGE
④ PARADE GROUND
⑤ ROSE GARDEN
⑥ PUNJAB ARTS COUNCIL
⑦ CRICKET STADIUM
⑧ GOVERNMENT PRESS BUILDING
⑨ TAGORE THEATRE
⑩ SHASTRI MARKET
⑪ BIRD SANCTUARY
⑫ HOTEL JW MARRIOT
⑬ HOCKEY STADIUM
⑭ DISTRICT COURT COMPLEX

following the strict hierarchy of the Seven Vs to create networks and flows is most conducive to the introduction of smart technologies for service delivery, transportation, and sustainability.

It is time that Chandigarh fights for something other than being a protected and preserved relic of modern town planning. While we may have missed the opportunity to extend the Smart City fabric into the region, it is important that the planning of the municipal limits of Chandigarh be done with great attention to detail. Otherwise, like the city of Jaipur and others that have historic walled cities at their core, the city of Chandigarh can be swallowed by its conurbation and become a threatened relic. The writing is on the wall when we see the green belts being taken over by development pressure, the peri-urban areas and urban villages filled with unsafe towers and gated communities, a complete reversal of the gains which Chandigarh makes through public infrastructure.

It is in this critical moment that Chandigarh finds itself. The architect and the urban planner need to assume the role of an urban surgeon—a metaphor that was dear to Corbusier—reassessing this growing patchwork of metropolis, and weaving it into a homogenous and aesthetically reasoned urban place. It is perhaps fortunate that Chandigarh has been preserved, for it now offers the opportunity to create a game-changing experience of urbanity. Neither Nehru nor Corbusier could have known that 60 years after their passing, the concept of Smart Cities would recover the essential smartness of their endeavor.

The Smart City of Chandigarh can execute an ambitious plan to replicate and scale the integrated interventions planned for Sectors 17, 22, 35 and 43, into the whole urban domain. By focusing all efforts on building the public infrastructure and the public space of the city, Chandigarh will temper its Smart City ambitions with the spirit of its Vision Statement: to become a leader in 'livability, sustainability, equality, and innovation.' While the goals to achieve this vision are pragmatic, they should not lose the poetry of the original ambition, which Corbusier captures in the 'Edict of Chandigarh':

> The city of Chandigarh is planned to human scale. It puts us in touch with the infinite cosmos and nature. It provides us with places and buildings for all human activities by which the citizens can live

a full and harmonious life. Here the radiance of nature and heart are within our reach.

This evocation of humanism is far removed from the crass futurism of the early Corbusier. It is more akin to the Corbusier who effusively remarked, after his first visit to Mumbai in 1949, a city brimming with colour, light and festivity, that architecture is primarily a 'backdrop for culture.'

In an age of symbols, it would be wise for Chandigarh to transform its approach to managing the heritage of public spaces. Let us look forward to a day when the collective performance of Yoga, for which the Capitol plaza was recently opened to public use, can happen on a daily basis along with other public activities, and every school child in the city can experience the sheer drama of architecture, the emblems of democracy writ large into an urban landscape against the backdrop of nature.

———

URBAN INDIA
Towards a Smart urban turn

Rahul Mehrotra

In India, the formalization of the 'Urban Turn' occurred with the Urbanization Commission that was appointed by the then Prime Minister Rajiv Gandhi in1986. The commission's mandate as defined in its document was that

> Urban India should, with utmost urgency, transform from merely being a concentration of population in towns into one, which is capable of generating economic growth in a sustained manner. The Planning Commission has been the apex body in the field of planning in India, but its orientation has been sectoral though not spatial. The National Commission on Urbanization (NCU) of 1986 is a precedent for asking such questions in previous generations. We look to it to identify useful shifts in our imagination of 'urban' within the Indian context.

It advocated for structural reforms to create an enabling environment for urban development in specific to the spatial structure of urbanization, regional land use and land-related policies, institutional structures and frameworks of governance, urban poverty, affordable housing, and finance and management. It also emphasized the importance of urban form and Heritage conservation—perhaps for the first time embedding these criteria in the official language of urban discourse in India.

The considerations that underlie NCU's proposals were the integration of economic and spatial planning; to promote an urbanization strategy to support both agricultural and industrial development; to support and assist the existing urban centres. 'Both to revive their economies and to upgrade their infrastructure', especially those which show economic growth potential and to totally negate the idea of starting new growth. One of the important outcomes was emphasizing the spatial dimensions of Urbanization. The commission stressed the

> creation of 329 new Generators of Economic Momentum (GEMs) and emphasizing the strengthening of larger metropolises. Classified cities based on economic momentum into National Priority Cities (Bombay, Madras, Delhi, Calcutta), State Priority Cities and 49 Spatial Priority Urbanization Regions (SPURs) and 555 settlements as centres of possible growth with the SPURs to have a special allocation of resources from centre and state.

So essentially for the first time the hierarchy of cities was seen and articulated in formal planning processes making for much more nuanced reading of the urban condition in India. Like most government documents of this nature, this report stayed largely below the radar as governments came and went—not paying attention to the urban time bomb India was sitting on!

Less than a decade later, India liberalized its economy in 1992. This accelerated not only the urbanization process but the presence of global capital for the first time in post independent India. In this post-liberalized economy, cities began to be characterized by physical and visual contradictions in a landscape charged with polarities. Furthermore with globalization and the emergence of a post-industrial service-based economy in Indian cities, urban space has been fragmented and polarized with the rich and poor jostling for access to amenities. By the late 1990s, the state had more or less given up the responsibility of projecting an 'idea of India' through the built and physical environment as it had done in the post-independence era with the several state capitals such as Chandigarh, Gandhinagar, Bhubaneswar, etc., and government and educational campuses such as the Indian Institutes of Technology across the country. Today the major state-directed projects are highways, flyovers, airports, telecommunications networks and electricity grids which connect urban centres but don't contribute to determining or guiding their physical structure.

Sector 17, Chandigarh
© Rajiv Kumar

In India's post-liberalization economy, cities and their burgeoning peripheries have become sites for the shifting of responsibilities and concurrently an evolving relationship between the private and the public. Today, private capital chooses to build environments that are insulated from their context, without the burdens of facilitating citizenship or place-making necessary in a real city. These gated communities take the form of vertical towers in the inner city and sprawling suburban compounds on the peripheries. In fact in the state-controlled economy the physical relationship between different classes was often orchestrated according to a master plan founded upon entitlement to housing and proximity to employment. In the new economy, the fragmentation of service and production locations has resulted in a new, bazaar-like urbanism that has woven its presence through the entire urban landscape.

With the retreat of the state in the 1990s (in different measures across India), the space of the 'everyday' became the place where economic and cultural struggles are articulated, and the physical shape cities in

India have taken manifests itself in the informal landscape of the bazaar city! This bazaar-like in form, or the kinetic city can be seen as the symbolic image of the emerging urban Indian condition. The processions, weddings, festivals, hawkers, street vendors and slum dwellers all create an ever-transforming streetscape—a city in constant motion where the very physical fabric is characterized by the kinetic. The Static City, on the other hand, dependent on architecture for its representation is no longer the single image by which the city is read. Thus architecture is not the 'spectacle' of the city nor does it even comprise the single dominant image of the city.

In this kinetic urbanism, Architecture is often not the only 'spectacle' upon which society relies to express its aspirations, nor does it even comprise the single dominant image of most Indian cities. Quite in contrast, festivals such as Diwali, Dussera, Navratri, Muharram, Durga

High rise apartment buildings and slums co-exist in Gurgaon
© Rajnish Wattas

Puja, Ganesh Chaturthi, and many more have emerged as the visual and representational spectacles of contemporary India. Their presence on the everyday landscape pervades and dominates the popular visual culture of India's cities, towns and villages. In fact, the increasing concentration of global flows in urban centres has exacerbated the inequalities and spatial divisions between social classes. In this context, an architecture or urbanism of equality in an increasingly inequitable economic condition requires a deeper consideration, so as to locate the wide range of places that signify and commemorate the cultures excluded from the spaces of global flows. Such places do not necessarily lie in the formal production of architecture, but often challenge it with a counterculture that takes on multiple forms. These are the landscapes of the self-help settlements often referred to as slums or the periphery of cities that grow outside the formal state-controlled urban limit. Similarly, the over 300 towns in India that are expected to become cities of one million people and more in the next two or three decades are actively producing forms of urbanism outside the mainstream discussion on architecture or urban planning and more importantly with no clear policy from the State.

In India today, hyper-consumption, fuelled by a rapidly growing economically mobile middle class, is resulting in the construction of a new landscape of global derivatives or the images of globalization. And it is an irony—that of the collusion of consciously dysfunctional land markets and exclusionary design and planning at multiple scales that has created a deeply conflicted fabric within which poorer communities have managed to survive, thrive and also alter and challenge the notion of formality! This is deeply challenged by the world-class city idea and slum free city imagination—often propelled by the government and financial institutions by a poorly informed appreciation of Dubai and Shanghai— the havens of impatient capital.

The architecture that results from this attitude often displays a complete detachment from its ambient environment as well as the place and community in which it is set. Furthermore, its tectonic quality and materiality is most often unmindful of local resources and traditions of building. Such architectural production is usually a quick response to large-scale infrastructure projects (such as upper income housing, hospitals, schools, colleges and commercial development) that allow private participation in otherwise largely government-controlled sectors.

Most importantly, this form of global architecture thrives on its perceived competence to provide predictable and stable services for (often impatient) capital searching for a host terrain in which to invest. Consequently, design services are often outsourced to Western firms perceived to be competent and well experienced in configuring global buildings—namely, those well versed in the use of new materials and technologies that meet international standards and facilitate the predictable value of the building's performance. This notion of design by a remote agency enhances, rather than diminishes, the perceived value of this form of global architecture.

In a bid to bring logic and perhaps coherence to this scenario, in 2015, the present government under the leadership of Prime Minister Narendra Modi announced a new initiative called the Smart City Mission. Interestingly this was announced six decades after Chandigarh and a decade after the report of the National Commissions on Urbanization in 1986. On the government's website this idea is defined in more detail and articulates that

> the key features of a Smart City are in the intersect between Competitiveness, Capital and Sustainability. The Smart Cities should be able to provide good infrastructure such as water, sanitation, reliable utility services, health care; attract investments; transparent processes that make it easy to run commercial activities; simple and on line processes for obtaining approvals, and various citizen centric services to make citizens feel safe and happy.

What does it really mean? The definition seems to cover everything: sustainable, transparent, good governance, efficiency—each term broad enough to be interpreted in its own way without commitment to any perceivable deliverable. The attributes of a Smart City, again as defined by the formal apparatus is that

> Smart Cities are projected to be equipped with basic infrastructure and will offer a good quality of life through smart solutions. Assured water and power supply, sanitation and solid waste management, efficient urban mobility and public transport, robust IT connectivity, e-governance and citizen participation along with safety of its citizens are some of the likely attributes of these Smart Cities.

Facing page:
A luxury hotel in Chandigarh
© Rajiv Kumar

Implicit in these definitions and official statements is underlying reliance on technology—as the silver bullet to solve all these pressing urban problems. That by networking infrastructure and people efficiencies could be potentially leveraged? If we accept that technology is seen as the silver bullet then the irony is that the one thing that characterizes or makes Planning in India unique globallys is that it stands precariously on an extremely thin layer of data! Invariably in most urban centres it's the non-governmental organizations and civil society more generally that often fills these data gaps for cities to operate. Furthermore 'data' in data driven cities is strangely apolitical; disconnected from the intent of use, the systems of use and users. Often controlled by foreign Consultants. In fact the rhetoric on Smart Cities and the imagination of their form as well as lifestyles they aspire to support, clearly ignores the reality of the messiness of Indian cities!

The obvious critiques of the Smart City range from its impulses to universal, in that these cities in their aspirations do not recognize geography, like coastal cities and in the Hills etc. Nor does it recognize the DNA of cities—temple towns, market towns, etc.

Does the idea of a Smart City actually have anything to do with cities? Or is it an abstract formulation of a terrain? Will Indian cities be like Chinese cities of the last two decades? Like Chinese cities, which are merely the best cities in China; generic cities in China—not Chinese cities.

The idea of a Smart City to a great extent is based on the belief of planners, city managers and now politicians that substantial and instrumental use of information and communication technologies in the management of urban functions can make cities work better! This discourse is clearly related to the aspiration or impulse to make their cities competitive in terms of revenues, jobs and to attract Capital. What is the purpose of the city—beyond capital accumulation? The Smart City shifts the discussion to cities as a business model rather than one of social justice.

Facing page:
Rajiv Gandhi IT Park,
Chandigarh
© Rajiv Kumar

And it is in this context that we should remember and learn from Chandigarh—a city of democracy or individual freedom. As the architect Romi Khosla has very clearly articulated:

171

> We have forgotten how Chandigarh was once the face of Fabians, Socialism and Egalitarian Modernism, planted on Indian soil to procure the freedom of the individual and then guarantee it through the three democratic Institutions: the legislature, judiciary, and the executive.

And in comparison he describes the Smart city, which is characterized by

> ...ease of personal access to technology, credit rating and legitimate pursuits of desire and comfort. And most importantly, Smart Cities being gated, provide the protection for the emergent middle class—a class that can earn substantial salaries, and live in safety to have some wealth without the need to supplement it from inheritance they never got...Only social and political compliance seems to be a precondition.

This comparison is emblematic of contemporary India. For the built landscape in India today symbolizes two simultaneous transitions at play in our political landscape—one a transition out of socialism and the other a transition into capitalism. In the simultaneous play of transitions such as these, the built environment is naturally a muddle with the fallouts of both transitions finding expression in the physical form of the cities. Ruptures in the urban fabric and startling adjacencies characterize the city that evolves with these narratives colliding in urban space. The two narratives or political rhetoric that then are put into play are those of 'building a global city' (the Singapore, Dubai and Shanghai models) or a city that panders to Global capital and that of a city which is about building a civil society or a city that supports lives. Clearly the narrative of the Smart City has merely supplemented the global city narrative, as it is essentially global capital dependent. And here technology is the Trojan Horse under which the rubric is constructed. The paraphernalia in each one of these cities is different. In the former the ground has to be prepared to allow capital to land softly and securely. In the other citizens are placed first and basic infrastructure and patterns of mobility determine how the city grows and how people have equitable access to these amenities. It is really the choice between these two directions or attitudes to city building that will be central to the discussion about the future of urban India.

In summary, City planning in India was pre-empted by rapid urbanization without the capacity to manage this incredible phenomenon. Thus in the last decades Planning followed growth not led it. Thus our capacity as a nation to deal with housing, which led to slums or inability to manage land markets, which led to unregulated real estate, will not be easy to reverse. Planning has become less speculative as a result and of course completely decimated by the myopia of our politicians. So Smart Cities if anything to be relevant to the India condition will need to harness radically altered understanding of public purpose and the common good. For the public interest by definition cities must be better planned. Smart Cities should make planning lead the way, become *Avant-Garde* once again and not be obsessed just with capital and technology but instead equally emphasize that cities should aspire to be humane centric in their conceptualization and formulation. At least what the rubric of Smart Cities has brought to the discussion in the political conversation in India is a focus on cities. This itself is finally a true urban turn and perhaps one premised more on the impulses to implement what the NCU achieved. Clearly an opportunity to bring the urban to centre stage and recognize this as a reality that is upon us in India. However, we should *not* be reinforcing what the politicians are saying that in 20 years we will have 100 Smart Cities—the slogan in India should be that in 20 years we will have a 100 great cities where Indians will lead better lives. This is where the aspirations and inspirations embedded in the ideal of Chandigarh are still relevant in India today!

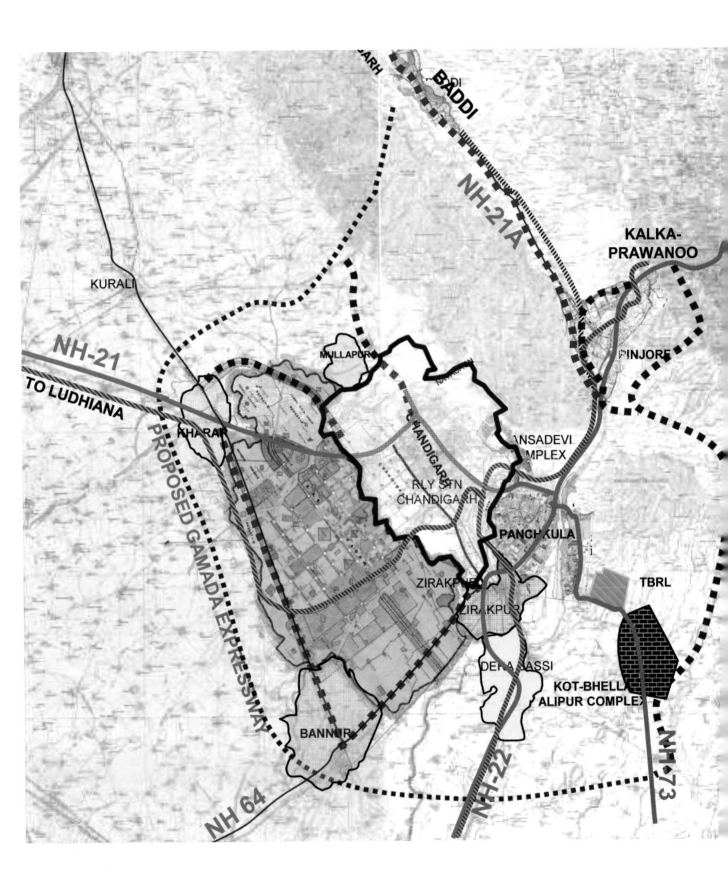

THE CHANDIGARH MASTER PLAN 2031
A vision for the future of the 'City Beautiful'

Sumit Kaur

The Chandigarh Plan prepared and implemented for the city in 1951, has had to face a quantum change geo-politically, socially, economically and because of the immediate abutting states of Punjab and Haryana. Chandigarh City, couched in an area identified as a Union Territory has been burdened with validating the original Plan as well as judiciously addressing the pressures of the new circumstances created around it. These pressures centre on population growth spurted by the towns of Mohali and Panchkula on its fringes (causing it to be nicknamed Tricity with the size of a metropolis); the City developing a Technology Park and the formation of slums. The villages engulfed in the urban fabric too pose questions about the appropriate modus of planning, development and regulatory mechanisms in the context of the City's future growth.

The City's future is rich with possibilities that can help it to achieve the 'Smart' tag, sustain its title of 'City Beautiful', and retain its environmental sensibility with its seamless greens, the background of the Shivalik Hills, the manmade Sukhna Lake and the massive afforestation efforts to keep it recharged. A city which can balance urban growth with ecology is truly a blessing on the planet and its future must ensure its continuity with that past. The cherry on the cake has been the recent tag of a World Heritage Site inscription by UNESCO to honour the Master Creator Le Corbusier's design of the Capitol Complex.

On 23rd April 2015, the Chandigarh Master Plan-2031 (CMP-2031) was duly notified. The visionary plan, showcases how Chandigarh, the first large experiment in Modern urbanism, now a brownfield site, despite its constraints and challenges, can continue to evolve into an efficient, inclusive, equitable, responsive, healthy, Smart and sustainable city. The CMP-2031 played a pivotal role in providing strength to the Nomination Dossier for the UNESCO World Heritage Status accorded to the city.

View of the Capitol Complex, Chandigarh
Picture Courtesy:
Chandigarh Tourism

To fully appreciate the significance of the Chandigarh Master Plan 2031 it is imperative that we cast a glance at the young city's chequered history from its very inception to the present day.

HISTORICAL PERSPECTIVE

In 1948, after a careful selection process, 70 sq. km of agricultural land dotted with villages, ponds and trees, was acquired in the picturesque foothills of the Shivalik mountains to make space for the new capital of Punjab, which had lost its capital city of Lahore following the Partition of

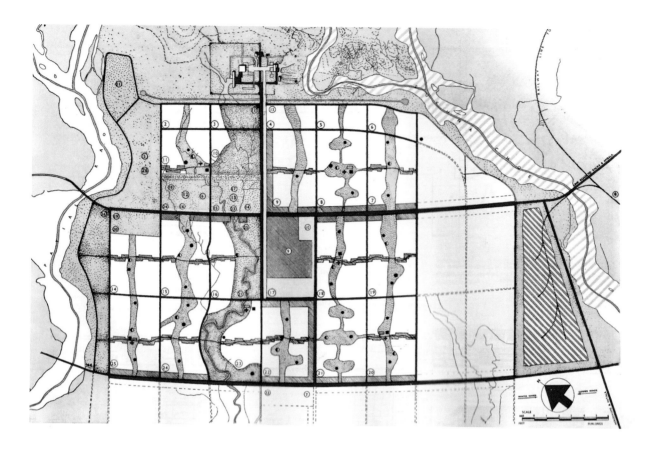

Corbusier's master plan for
phase I of Chandigarh
© FLC-ADAGP

India. The plan was to have the city house a population of 5 lakh (half a million) people. The task for preparing the plan for Chandigarh was first assigned to the American planner Albert Mayer, who developed the initial plan, but could not continue work due to the death of his partner Mathew Nowicki.

Le Corbusier, the Swiss-born French architect-planner was then commissioned by Pandit Jawaharlal Nehru, Independent India's first Prime Minister, to prepare the Master Plan for Chandigarh. The brief to the architect by him was

> Let this be a new town, symbolic of freedom of India unfettered by the traditions of the past...an expression of the nation's faith in the future.

Le Corbusier's Plan—1951

Corbusier's Plan was based on the celebrated CIAM (Congrès Internationaux d' Architecture Moderne) theories focusing on four major

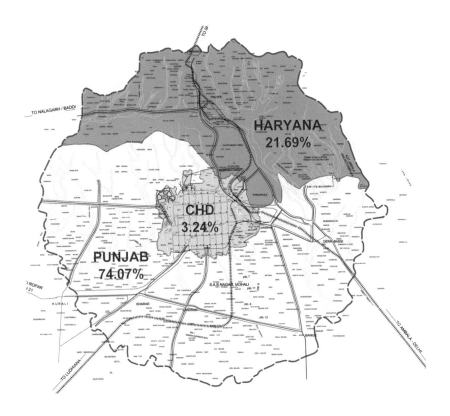

Left:
Periphery plan showing Punjab
and Haryana (16 km)-Model
Photo courtesy: Department of
Urban Planning, Chandigarh

Below:
Regional plan of Chandigarh
Photo courtesy: Department of
Urban Planning, Chandigarh

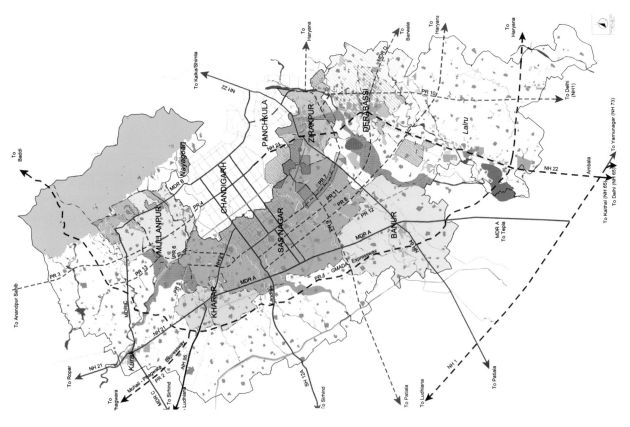

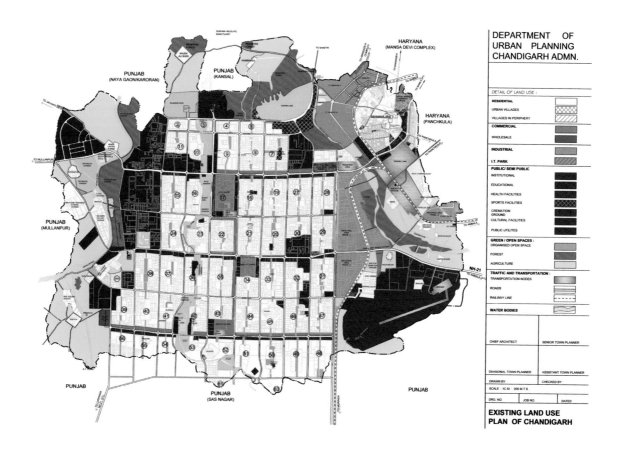

Chandigarh's existing land use plan
Photo courtesy:
Department of Urban Planning, Chandigarh

city functions: Living, Working, Care of Body & Spirit and Circulation. With the silhouette of the Shivalik hills forming the backdrop and Patiali ki Rao and Sukhna Choe, the two natural rivulets, defining the eastern and western boundaries, the grid iron plan, designed for fast traffic, created a matrix of introvert, self-sufficient, walkable neighbourhood units/ Sectors. The main administrative functions of the city—the executive, the legislative and the judiciary—were housed in the Capitol Complex— the symbolic 'Head', the City Centre in its 'Heart', while the Industrial Area and the Panjab University formed the eastern and western limbs of the city. The N-Choe, a small seasonal rivulet meandering across the city was beautifully integrated into the City Plan to form the major lung of the city.

Chandigarh's 'Green City' concept, distribution of population based on the administrative pecking order, and the low-rise low density development were features that helped maintain a certain qualitative aspect to the city. High-rise construction was ruled out due to budgetary constraints and non-acculturation of the people to high-rise living. The Plan envisioned an unperturbed city growth by limiting its expansion through strategising Periphery Control which later became an Act.

Periphery Controlled Area: To safeguard the city from unplanned and unregulated growth, an 8 km stretch, which was later extended to 16 km around the urban area, was earmarked as green and agricultural area, and brought under the Panjab New Capital (Periphery) Control Act, 1952.

A deviation to the Periphery Control Act occurred in 1966 on account of the 'Reorganization of the State of Punjab' as a result of which the city became the common capital of two states, Haryana (having been carved out from Punjab) as well as Punjab. Subdivision of the 16 km periphery left Chandigarh confined within its 3.3% share, and land being a state subject, the city had no control on Punjab's share of 75% and Haryana's share of 21.7%. Planned townships started showing up soon after, with Haryana's Panchkula and Punjab's Mohali townships becoming prized accomplishments for their respective States. Both states have aggressively moved forward to continue urban growth at a significant scale with Punjab and Haryana adding around 12 new settlements into the planning framework. It is anticipated that the combined population of all these satellite towns along with Chandigarh may peak to a daunting 4.5 million by 2031.

DEVELOPMENT STATUS OF CHANDIGARH AS UNION TERRITORY

Le Corbusier's Master Plan 1951 for Chandigarh was a two-phase plan for housing a 5 lakh population; the first phase for accommodating 1.5 lakh (1 lakh equals 100,000). The prime urban characteristics for both phases created an extensively green, low-rise low-density city with state of art social and physical infrastructure; making it an attractive destination and a novel way of community living. The first phase was completely urban whereas in the second phase, villages got incorporated. Due to aforementioned circumstances the city experienced unprecedented growth forcing the administration to carve out a third phase of additional sectors for residential use while retaining controls for the earlier ones. Densification however took place with single units serving multiple families along with time to time relaxation in FAR/Ground coverage etc., for allowing need based changes in all land uses. Subsequently with increased urbanisation slums started forming depriving the poor of decent habitation for qualitative living. Villages began to take the brunt of several activities and unmet demand for cheap housing, warehousing, non-formal commerce and industry etc., dotting the spatially ordered city with sporadically located illegal, unsafe, incompatible, highly dense and encroachment-riddled built environment. Inability to deal with this massive urban growth resulted in a knee-jerk reaction by adjusting many of the city functions across its natural borders of the Patiali-ki-Rao and the Sukhna Choe.

With a great momentum for growth but limited scope for horizontal expansion in its physical boundary of 114 square kilometres, this landlocked city is beginning to buckle under increased population growth (10.54 lakh as per Census 2011). Pressures owing to traffic congestion, infrastructure stress, reducing greens by diversion in use, building violation and several other factors are causing damage to the original concept considered sacrosanct.

INITIATION AND PREPARATION OF THE MASTER PLAN (CMP-2031)

The Chandigarh Administration constituted an Expert Committee to prepare a Master Plan taking cognisance of the skewed development taking place. The geographical area of the first comprehensive plan for the city included the almost fully developed 70 sq km of the area planned by Le Corbusier, the 44 sq km of its 3% share of the 16 km Periphery Controlled Area, the 23 villages (6 within sector grids and 17 in the Periphery), and the Census Town of Mani Majra.

The focus of CMP 2031 was primarily:

- ► An assessment of the existing situation and the issues thereof
- ► Vision for future development
- ► Key Strategies
- ► Guidelines for Plan monitoring.

Public participation of stakeholders, experts and eminent visionaries ensured a healthy consultation process. A SWOT Analysis helped formulate and consolidate city problems, demands and aspirations leading to the Chandigarh Vision. The Draft Plan on which Objections and Suggestions were invited from citizens were considered by a Board of Inquiry and Hearing as well as by the Chandigarh Administration and the Final Master Plan sent to Government of India for approval.

CHANDIGARH MASTER PLAN 2031 (CMP–2031) HIGHLIGHTS

The CMP–2031 is intended to create a sustainable future for the City whilst conserving and maintaining its manmade and natural heritage. Aligned with the Government of India's (GOI's) Action Plan for Climate Change, the Solar Energy Mission, the Enhanced Energy Efficiency Mission, the Sustainable Habitat Mission and, the Mission for Conserving Water and Creating Green India, the Plan will help generate the correct ethos for the City's sustainable future.

The essence of the original concept is intended to be retained by respecting the historical legacy of its acclaimed Circulation System, the

Chandigarh's enlisted heritage-heritage zones Photo courtesy: Department of Urban Planning, Chandigarh

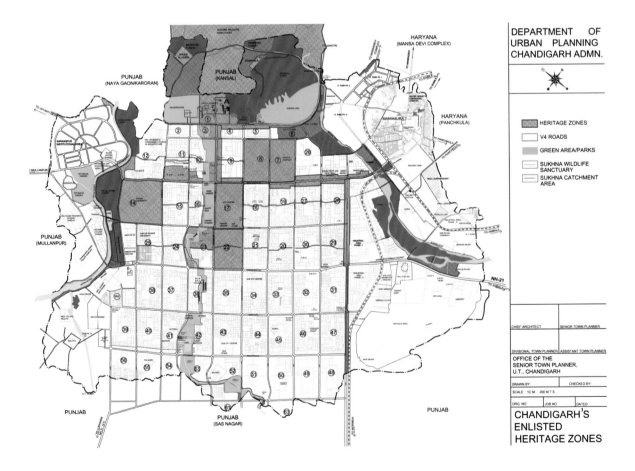

Green lung Spaces, its scenic backdrop of the Shivaliks with the prized Capitol Complex in the foreground. The GOI's approval of the report by the Expert Heritage Committee lends credence to the Preservation, Conservation, Management and Maintenance of Chandigarh's Heritage, and due recognition of delineating Heritage Zones, Precincts, Buildings, Natural features and Vistas. The First Phase Sectors (1–30) have been titled the 'Corbusian Sectors' and are required to retain low–rise low–density governed by Heritage Regulations for the city's Enlisted Heritage categorised by their significance, as, Grade l, 2 and 3.

The area north of the Capitol Complex, sacred from the urban design perspective, falls in Heritage Zone 1 and is to remain a No Construction Zone in line with the Edict of Chandigarh. Accordingly the CMP–2031 has proposed areas around villages falling within the city limit to be retained as green agricultural or forest land. However as controls do not apply on abutting regions of Punjab and Haryana, the foothills of Shivaliks falling in the area are being subjected to rampant insensitive development violating the very essence of the original intent.

There is an urgent need for Preparation of a Metropolitan Plan amidst three independently governed territories for attaining balanced integrated sustainable development in the region with emphasis on connectivity and road network, airport development, green cover and zonation for Agriculture, Disaster Management, Financial and Governance issues for a combined Metropolitan Region, and safeguards for ecology-environment-heritage.

With the Sectoral grids nearly fully built of their designated land use, judicious use of the remainder miniscule 3101.9 acres of undeveloped land (in 17 scattered pockets) has been proposed after detailed stocktaking to meet the essential requirements of the city. Two pockets of land have been left as 'Reserved' for future unforeseen use. Optimum utilisation of the available land within the Sectoral grid along with qualitative improvements, have been proposed to enable the city to move ahead with the times while maintaining its inherent character.

The City's Holding Capacity for Perspective Year 2031 has been projected at 16 lakhs. A population of 10 lakhs are to be accommodated in residential sectors of Phases 1, 2 and 3, whilst the remaining 6 lakhs shall be accommodated in the periphery areas. Balance may have to be diverted to the surrounding region through Policy/Strategy at the interstate level.

Housing for All incorporates the variety of options prevalent in Chandigarh, (private, public, co-operative group housing, high-end and low cost, etc.) though without a systematic evaluation of housing demand. CMP–2031 has suggested a 'Holistic Housing Policy Framework for addressing unmet and past aberration in demand. Since land resources are limited its optimal utilisation is a necessity. Plotted development has been ruled out and Group housing has been mandated with a rider that 15% units be reserved for Economically Weaker Sections (EWS); Government housing to cater for resident-domestic help. Already identified government housing pockets are to be redeveloped/reutilised and provision for hostels, student homes, elderly, night shelters or appropriate arrangements for informal sector to be made. Though slums have been on the government

Land use proposals of 17 pockets in the periphery
Photo courtesy: Department of Urban Planning, Chandigarh

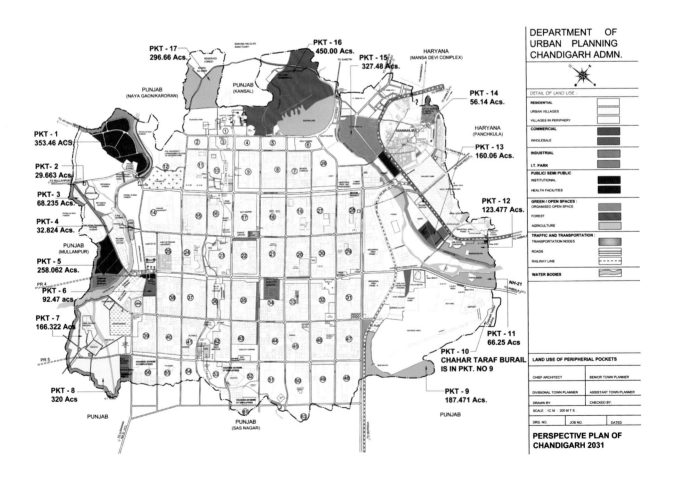

agenda since the 1970s much more is to be done to implement the Vision of a 'Slum-free' city. A proposal to execute, on 18 identified sites, the formulated 'Chandigarh Small Flats Scheme-2006' has been suggested.

The Capitol Complex has had to multi-task for three government entities: the Chandigarh Administration, Punjab Government, and the Haryana government distressing the buildings' functional requirements. Spaces allocated to the two governments have fallen short, resulting in additions and alterations derogatory to the overall ambience of all the noteworthy buildings constituting the Capitol Complex with the High Court Building accruing an intense increase in the number of court rooms and ancillary buildings. The Heritage Status of the Capitol Complex prohibits any additional buildings be built in the nominated property of the Complex. Gaps in infrastructure shall be addressed in identified vacant institutional pockets through a holistic planning proposal taking into consideration future requirements. While the essential requirements of the two states shall be met within the city, the other offices and directorate offices are proposed to be shifted to the new towns being developed by the states adjoining the city.

Commercial Centres to keep pace with the emerging shopping trends:

Large undeveloped commercial areas—City Centre Sector 17, Sub City Centres in Sectors 34 and 43, commercial belts along major roads, neighbourhood shopping centres are to be developed with new planning concepts to enable greater flexibility of space, integrated state of the art services and provision for underground parking etc. Urban renewal and streetscaping of existing commercial areas—invigorating them with incidental shopping, street vending zones, food courts, amphitheatre etc., for 'Place Making' is needed. Additional FAR to existing commercial centres is not recommended, however holistic review of architectural controls to address modern requirements has been proposed. For Warehousing, Transport Area and Bulk Material Market land has been proposed to decongest areas of the city where unplanned development has taken place.

Multi-Storied Mixed Use Development along the 7.2 km stretch of Vikas Marg (with commercial on the lower floors and institutional/residential use above), has been proposed as a departure from the architecturally

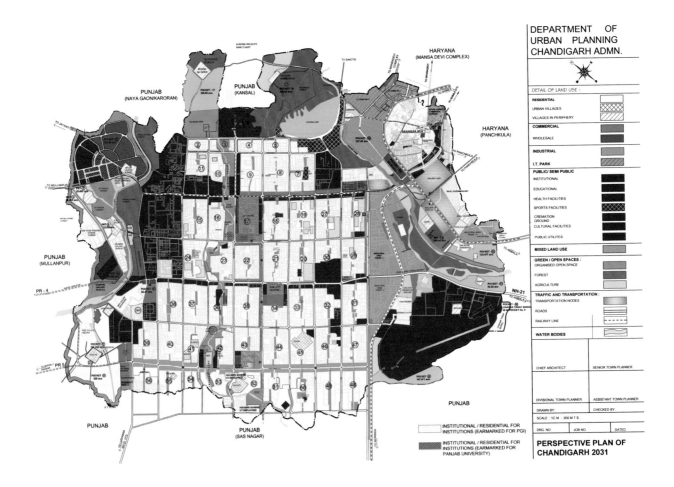

Perspective plan 2031
Photo courtesy: Department of
Urban Planning, Chandigarh

controlled units and gated communities. The recommendation has been made to optimise the only major undeveloped area within the sectoral grid besides creating a strong urban design statement at the edge of the Phase II sectors designed by Le Corbusier.

To maintain the high order of the social infrastructure and the quality of life of the city residents, gaps identified in the hierarchical range of city-level and Sector-level educational, medical, cultural facilities shall be plugged in through quantitative and qualitative upgradation to ensure adequacy and equitable distribution. Augmentation of dispensaries, hospitals, high schools, colleges, fire stations, religious buildings, hostel accommodation and guest facilities, night shelters for the homeless, crèches, *anganwari*s and old people's homes have been recommended. Space auditing of large institutional campuses, concept of sharing of facilities, use of modern technology and E-governance is recommended for optimum utilization and to keep the city abreast with latest requirements.

To facilitate expansion of regional level premier institutes like Post Graduate Institute of Medical Education and Research and the Panjab University, additional institutional land has been proposed in the periphery. Land has been earmarked along the Chandigarh Kalka Highway for new colleges, health care institutes, etc.

Recommendations for development of a Cultural Hub in Sector 42, Nehru Centre for Performing Arts, Permanent Exhibition Centre, and Second Phase of Kala Gram—a regional cultural centre, and other city level facilities have been made to append the cultural infrastructure.

Comprehensive Urban Renewal of the Industrial Area Phase I and Phase II

These areas are witnessing a host of problems like stress on infrastructure, traffic congestion, incompatibility of land use and disorderly urban design after the concessions of change of trade from industrial to commercial, additional FAR and height permitted to large industrial plots. The undeveloped area of the Industrial Area Phase III has been proposed for intensive utilisation as flatted service factories and for modern warehousing. Large scale industries are to be adjusted in the region in view of the constraint of space within the landlocked city.

Rajiv Gandhi IT Park,
Chandigarh
© Rajiv Kumar

To give further boost to the Information and Technology, additional 250 acres adjoining the Phase 1 and Phase II of the Rajiv Gandhi Information and Technology Park has been proposed as IT Phase III along with ancillary and other related uses.

Open spaces have been recommended as Inviolable Land Use to prevent them from being stifled and diverted to other land uses. Enhancing the qualitative and quantitative green through sensitive interventions, additional green areas, forest areas and agricultural land has been proposed. Green belts have been proposed along the interstate boundary and along major approach roads to enhance the visitor experience and image of the city.

A Comprehensive Mobility Plan for the Chandigarh Urban Complex comprising of Chandigarh, Mohali, Panchkula with linkages to other towns has been proposed to improve intercity and intra-city movements. The integrated multimodal mass rapid transport system, with metro, commuter rail, BRTS, feeder buses, non-motorised vehicles minimizing travel time and ensuring maximum safety and comfort has been recommended to reduce dependence on personal vehicles. Due to heritage considerations, underground metro has been proposed within the sectoral grid. Additional road linkages to Panchkula and upcoming towns have been earmarked and recommendations for integrated Planning of ring roads to divert unwanted traffic passing through Chandigarh, direct connectivity to the new International Airport Terminal from Chandigarh side and upgradation of the Chandigarh Railway Station have been made. In addition, proposals for improvement of road geometrics, junctions and construction of underpasses have been recommended for seamless flow of traffic.

Chandigarh is to be promoted as a pedestrian and cycle friendly city with footpaths and cycle tracks and dedicated lanes completed to ensure safe and comfortable last mile connectivity. Concept of Park and Ride linked with MRTS shall be introduced to mainstream cycle as a mode of transport. Walking and cycling for leisure is also recommended through longitudinal Green corridors stretching across the city and offering varied spatial experiences, integrating cultural and recreational areas/natural features of the city.

For sustainable development of the city, an integrated approach to manage water supply, water treatment, storm water management and

Facing page:
Comprehensive mobility
plan—MRTS corridors
Photo courtesy:
Department of Urban
Planning, Chandigarh

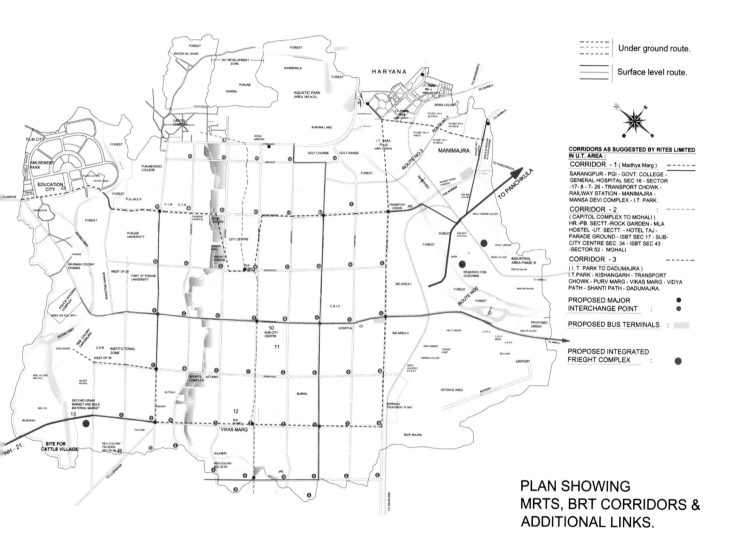

PLAN SHOWING
MRTS, BRT CORRIDORS &
ADDITIONAL LINKS.

sewerage management has been proposed. Entire city is to be based on canal water supply since tapping water from the deep confined aquifers is not desirable in view of Chandigarh's declining water table. To reduce consumption of potable water mandatory use of recycled water for all non-potable uses for buildings with an area of more than 2000 sq. mts, and provision of decentralised sewerage systems has been proposed for large campuses to enable use of tertiary treated water at source in addition to mandatory rain water harvesting for all institutions and residential units above one kanal (500 sq. yds). Recharging deep soil aquifers by harvesting rainwater through structures along the storm water drain network and integrated implementation of sustainable urban drainage systems (SUDS) have been advocated.

Chandigarh is being developed as a Solar City under the National Mission of Solar Energy as per which 25 MW large solar PV based power plant shall be developed in Patiala ki Rao Choe, 10 MW through solar PV based rooftop power generation to enable each house in the city to produce enough power for its domestic requirement. Installation of solar-based LED traffic lights, solar street lights, building integrated solar Photo Voltaic, SCADA based power monitoring of street lights and laying of underground 11 KV and 66 KV lines has been recommended.

Land for a new dumping ground has been earmarked near the existing dumping ground which is nearly fully exhausted. To minimise pollution the site has been enclosed within a green belt, however the CMP–2031 cautions that this is not an ideal arrangement. Since no other suitable site is available within the city limits, the Government of Punjab has been requested to identify 100 acres for a new dumping ground within their State. Simultaneously, the Chandigarh Administration shall need to minimise waste that goes to the dumping ground by introducing innovate decentralised ways based on concept of 'Reduce, Recycle and Reuse' to manage and treat waste.

To take the Neighbourhood concept to another level of sustainability and self sufficiency, Sectors/clusters of Sectors shall be retrofitted into fully close looped settlements which power themselves and handle their own waste. Adaptation of green building concepts shall be made mandatory in all future developments of Chandigarh. Some recommendations for protecting the ecological and environmental assets of Chandigarh are:

Facing page:
Securing catchment area of the Sukhna Lake
Photo courtesy: Department of Urban Planning, Chandigarh

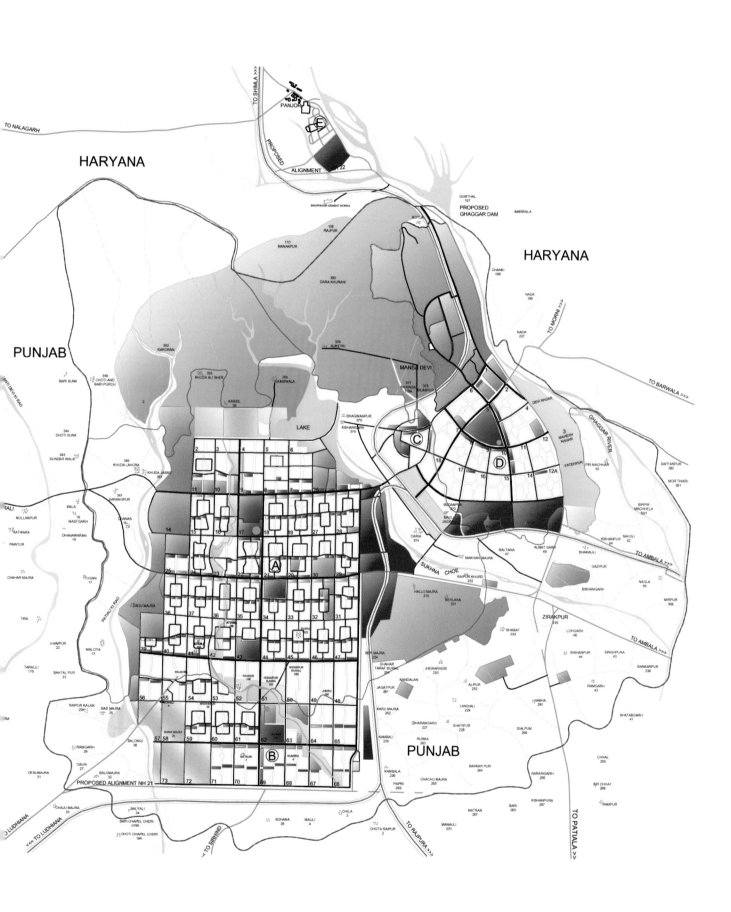

HARYANA

PUNJAB

TO NALAGARH

TO SHIMLA >>>

PANJORE

E

PROPOSED ALIGNMENT NH 22

BHURINDER CEMENT WORKS

GUMTHAL 197

PROPOSED GHAGGAR DAM

AMBWALA

KOTLA

108 RAJPUR

110 MANAKPUR

390 DARA KHURANI

HARYANA

CHANKU 198

NADA 199

TO MORNI >>>

TO BARWALA >>>

376 SUKETRI

362 KARORAN

363 KHUDA ALI SHER

388 JAMIDWALA

BARI SUNK

349 CHOTI AND BARI PURCH

KARSIL 26

2

NADA 227

MANSA DEVI

377 BHAINSA TIBA

378 NALAGARH

DEVI NAGAR

6

2

4

3 MANESH NAGAR

GHAGGAR RIVER

DAFFARPUR 360

BHAGWANPUR 375

KISHANGARH 375

C

7

9

12

5

11

D

FATEHPUR

PIR NACHHAR 53

MOR THIKRI 361

344 CHOTI SUNK

345 SUNDER WALA

348 KHUDA LAHORA

347 KHUDA JASSU 361

347 SARANGPUR

LAKE

2

3

4

5

6

18

17

16

15

14

12A

BIPPIR MACHHELA 53/1

KISHANPUR 54

SAHOLI 52

DHANAS 16

1

10

9

8

BUDANPUR 372

MALLI JAGIR

BALTANA 47

ALMAT GARH 49

DHAKAULI

GAZIPUR

TO AMBALA >>>

MALA

16 MASTGARH

DHANAWARAN 18

14

15

16

17

18

19

27

28

DARA 374

SUKHNA CHOE

MAKHAN MAJRA

NAGLA 55

MULLANPUR

RATWARA

PAINTUR

A

25

24

23

22

21

20

30

29

HALLO MAJRA 219

RAIPUR KHURD 232

SEHLANA 231

BISHANGARH

MIRPUR 356

COGAN 17

DADU MAJRA

36

37

36

35

34

33

32

31

ATTAWA

ZIRAKPUR 235

BHABAT 233

LOHGARH 48

CHAHAR MAJRA

TIRA

MALOYA 13

39

40

41

42

43

44

45

46

47

BURAIL 102

BISHANPUR 44

SINGHPURA 43

JHAMPUR 22

BAHTAL PUR 23

PALSORA

KAJHER 108

HAZABPUR KLAERA 105

BIDANPUR BURAIL 109

JHARU 107

BIR MAJRA

CHAHAR TARAF BURAIL

JHEWARHERI 283

ALIPUR 252

BISHANPUR 44

RAMGARH 42

BANKARPUR 236

TARAULI 175

56

55

54

53

52

51

50

49

48

JAGATPUR 281

KANDALAN

LANDIALU 229

NABHA 290

SHATABGARH 41

RAIPUR KALAN 294

BAD MAJRA 25

BRONDI 19

KARU MAJRA 262

SHATIPUR 228

DIALPUM 269

DESUMAJRA 31

DAUN 27

57

58

59

60

61

62

63

64

65

JHARMANGARH 226

RURKA 263

CHACHU MAJRA 288

BANKAR PUR 264

NARAINGARH 286

CHHAL 285

RAMGARH 29

BALOMAJRA 32

SHAHI MAJRA

MATAUR 6

B

KAMBALI 225

KAMBALA 226

PAPRI 289

BIR CHHAT 286

PROPOSED ALIGNMENT NH 21

73

72

71

70

69

68

67

66

PUNJAB

CHAJU MAJRA 33

BALYALI 34

SOHANA 35

MALLI

CHILA 3

CHOTA RAIPUR 2

TO RAJPURA >>>

MANAULI 270

MATRAN 267

BARI 262

KISHANPURA 267

RAMPUR

TO PATIALA >>>

TO LUDHIANA <<<

CHOTI CHAPEL CHERI 194

SARI CHAPEL CHERI 195

TO SIRHIND >>>

- Securing the entire catchment of the Sukhna Lake.
- Notifying an eco-sensitive zone (ESZ) around the Sukhna Wildlife Sanctuary.
- Proper protection of the Patiala-ki-Rao Choe and the Sukhna Choe to maintain their ecological integrity and natural drainage functions.
- Afforestation of 1.4 km stretch of agricultural land separating the Sukhna Lake Reserve forest and the Sukhna Wildlife Sanctuary to create a wildlife corridor for the safe to and fro movement of the wildlife.
- Declaring the area on the North of the Capitol Complex as a No Development Zone to maintain the green and natural backdrop of the city.

For sustainable integration of villages into the urban fabric, development plans for all the villages shall be drawn after undertaking detailed surveys to understand their unique character, respect the history and preserve and maintain the best features. Adequate provision for community facilities, open spaces, agro/village industry based economic activity, shall be made for the villages in the periphery, for which area around existing settlements has been identified. Use of solar energy, bio gas plants, rainwater harvesting, augmenting green spaces and green building concepts shall be promoted to create energy efficient model villages. Villages on the Shivalik foothills near Sukhna Wildlife Sanctuary shall be nurtured as Eco Sensitive villages.

Chandigarh falls within the Seismic Zone IV and as such has high risk from earthquakes. A pan city systematic examination of the structural safety of non-engineered buildings is required to guide follow up action for redevelopment, retrofitting, urban renewal, besides regular monitoring to check illegal construction and enforcement of Earthquake Resistant New Construction. Regular review and upgradation of the Disaster Management Plan is required.

CONCLUSION

In conclusion it is prudent to crystallise the concept of SUSTAINABILITY from its several interpretations drawn from ecological, social, economic, environmental or developmental parameters for protecting life and human options, using environmentally sound technologies, placing a real value on natural resources and creating a participative community building social structure--to a more focussed goal. Just as ecosystems move from young to mature state, Chandigarh is moving from a young urban system to a mature one; that is expected to have several functional niches, interconnections, competition, predation, succession with a qualitative and quantitative shift in use of energy, material resources, space, information, technology, etc.

The path adopted shall be of ACTIONS that help strengthen values knowledge technology, institutions etc., so that specific objectives are achieved that help Improve well-being of people and ecosystems. Rightfully the Smart City focus can help in achieving it.

It is hoped that this statutory document shall serve as a guiding spirit for city's all round development. Upholding the city's legacy, a quote from the Edict of Chandigarh seems most befitting once again 'The seed of the city is well sown, it is for the citizens to see that the tree flourishes.'

FROM THE ARCHIVES

CORBUSIER'S BRAVE NEW WORLD

Personal impressions

P.L. Varma

In order to appreciate Le Corbusier's creation one has to understand his philosophy. Born into an intensely devout family, it is apparent that religion played an important part in his subconscious, making the pursuit of truth his lifelong goal. To understand in depth what truth connotes and what it can lead to, he spent time contemplating and meditating and even chose to live with his wife in silence and quiet in a tiny shack on the Mediterranean for six weeks in a year. In his search for truth, he went to the extent of closing down his office and stopping all communication with the world outside: even telegrams were not received by him. His habits were simple—he ate dinner with a fisherman living close by whom he then rewarded by designing a mural on the wall of his house, and he swam three times a day in the ocean under the blue Mediterranean sky which provided him the environment to meditate. Here, he lived in self-imposed discipline, not very different from that of a sanyasi in India, who lives a life of a recluse in a forest.

It is in this ambience that he conceived a new civilization, with a new architecture, new idioms of space and building relationships, all integrated with nature. Le Corbusier lived a serious life unfettered by the superficial pleasures of present day society. Such pleasures, to an Indian seeker of truth, are ephemeral and destructive of human happiness. Happiness, the aim of human existence on this earth can be won by truth, self-discipline, integral knowledge, and a life of purity when the inner and the outer self react on each other harmoniously. Corbusier's life speaks of the validity of this very theme of existence and his creations impart an ineffable sense of perfection. Evidently, the uncompromising pursuit of truth was an abiding theme in his work and philosophy—truth of design, materials and of colours—the truth of the Open Hand.

In his concept of the 'Brave New World', he did not let personal national and traditional predilections predominate. His creations were placed on a universal base with a common denominator—catering to the modern needs of mankind. India had a silent, oriental, almost spiritual appeal for him, in the midst of his predominantly occidental culture and background. This was confirmed when he showed Mr P.N. Thapar and me a book on India's civilization which he carried with him at one of his meetings with us in Paris.

The concept of the Capitol Complex in Chandigarh reveals Corbusier's approach to his philosophy of the livability of man. The various elements and symbols built into each of these structures are reflective of his philosophy of human existence which reaches out to the eternal in man. Each of the structures expresses the integral features of his philosophy, such as sacrifice, non-violence, justice and so on.

The Martyrs Memorial symbolizes gratitude and is a reminder of the principles of sacrifice. It is meant to instil courage to live and die for one's principles and attain immortality.

The Open Hand, conceived by Le Corbusier in 1943 when Hitler's military fist had imposed unlimited atrocities on Parisians, expresses non-violence. The Open Hand cannot hold a weapon. It is indicative of man's need to be free from greed. 'With a full hand I have received, with a full hand I give.' It is very apt that he thought of locating this symbol in India where his spiritual thoughts could be readily understood.

The High Court building (Temple of Justice) symbolizes three ideas in its structure—the majesty of law, the shelter of law and the power and fear of law. The magnificent entrance consisting of three monumental size columns reaching the roof expresses the majesty of law. The 7.6 sq m vaulted cantilevered roof provides the feel of shelter and a small serpent fountain at the entrance signifies the fear and power of law. (In

Facing page:
Le Corbusier with P.L. Varma and Pierre Jeanneret
© FLC-ADAGP

India serpent power is considered to be a universal power for sublimating human consciousness into the divine.)

The Assembly Hall has a form where walls also become a part of the roof and sunlight pours in through a bouchon cone on top to light up the hall. Infinity is not shut out by a roof but is brought into the hall. The clouds of sound absorbing element, apart from serving as an acoustic material, are meant to be a reminder of the blessings of rain. Corbusier conceived of an idea where the table of The Speaker would be illuminated by a shaft of sunlight at the start of the assembly session. This concept unfortunately could not materialize as Le Corbusier died soon after the opening of the building.

The Secretariat building is a workshop of administration. Happily, along its length, there are no enclosed corridors with shut doors on both sides as is normal in such buildings. The inside opens very frequently to the outside in its length and that too very gracefully. The roof provides a space for eating from where one gets a fantastic view of the majestic Himalaya. Here I must recall an incident of interest. Le Corbusier was going up a ramp when he saw some donkeys coming down. Aghast, he asked me, 'What is this?' When I told him that they were cranes for lifting the material to the various floors for building purposes, I remember he said, 'Wonderful! Wonderful!' He stood in silence for a while and when we started walking up he said, 'In India the lower world of animals and man worked together to create a building.' One day he wanted to paint murals on the walls of the ramp but unfortunately this could not be accomplished during his life time. I hope some eminent painter will fulfil his wish which postulates this affinity between man and the lower living world.

The Governor's Palace was a grand concept, where the sovereignty of the state needed a majestic appearance. Unfortunately the Lilliputian thoughts of some individuals and the chronic poverty of the Indian mind did not rise to the occasion to give a dignified edifice to the concept. When this happened, Corbusier quickly replaced it by the 'House of Knowledge' where all human activities, urban and rural could be analysed and researched into by experts and transmitted to the world as a new rhythm of knowledge with fresh idioms of social livability. Even this concept regrettably has not taken shape.

Chandigarh, Peaceful Moment
by the Sukhna Lake, which
was conceived due to the
foresight of P.L. Varma
© William J.R. Curtis, 2013

The Tower of Shadows is a study of the sun's shadows. Its monumentality obstructs the view of all that this complex expresses. To go beyond the shadows which is the creation of the sun itself is the aim of life. The size of the tower expresses the magnitude of shadowed ignorance in the world and the need to go beyond it. The whole complex, however, remains an unfinished ensemble, and to that extent takes away from the grandeur of the original design. The onenesss of the concept is lost and with it the power to understand the eternity of life which the whole conceptual display of the various elements meant to signify and emphasize.

These few words have been written in the memory of Le Corbusier to commemorate his birth centenary—a tribute to a man from a friend. The universality of Le Corbusier's spirit cannot be expressed in mere words. Corbusier has become a principle from which the rest of the world can learn.

Reproduced from: *Architecture + Design. Sept-Oct 1987.*
Courtesy: *Architecture + Design.*

LE CORBUSIER AS I KNEW HIM

M.N. Sharma

Since the advent of modern architecture, Le Corbusier has been considered one of its founding fathers. Today, he is regarded as the 20th century's greatest architect. What is fascinating about Le Corbusier is that, as time goes by, his works appear more meaningful and ageless. Le Corbusier's creative endeavours emanated from a passionately attentive, painstaking study of the world including both contemporary reality and the heritage of tradition and laws of nature. Paying tribute to Le Corbusier, Pandit Jawaharlal Nehru said,

> I have welcomed very greatly one experiment in India demonstrated in Chandigarh. Many people argue about it. Some like it and some dislike it. It is the biggest example in India of experimental architecture. It hits you on the head and makes you think. You may squirm at the impact but it makes you think. I do not like every building in Chandigarh. I like some of them very much. I like the general conception of the township very much but, above all, I like the creative approach not being tied down to what has been done by our forefathers, but thinking in new terms like air and ground, water and human beings.

Le Corbusier was not unaware of his place in history. By self-training, he was an environmentalist, painter, sculptor, architect, planner, poet, philosopher and a writer. Even though he influenced world thought on

contemporary planning and architecture, he faced many setbacks in
his early years. He was totally disciplined and even during the most
disappointing periods of his life, he relied on his inner strength. He
wrote in 1934, 'The defeats of past years represented as many victories.
Public opinion when aroused will force the same officials to change their
attitudes.' His predictions came true and all his sketches and unrealized
works are today published and held in very high esteem. Le Corbusier was
at the apex of his career when he accepted the challenging assignment
of designing Chandigarh.

During his second visit to India in 1951, Le Corbusier was fascinated by the sculptural forms of hand-made mud houses of the Punjab villages, the hard-working peasants and joyful children who lived in them. He admired their use of the materials at hand to create beauty and the play of light and shadow. He commented,

> At the end of 1951 in Chandigarh; possible contact with the essential delights of Hindu philosophy: fraternity between cosmos and living beings; stars, all of nature, sacred animals, birds, monkeys and cows and in the villages, the children, the adults and the still active old people, the pond and the mangroves, everything has an absolute presence and smiles: everything is miserably poor but well proportioned...

Le Corbusier used some of the motifs of these buildings in the Capitol Complex. These villages have all but disappeared, rebuilt in the rush to 'modernise'. Village houses, though inanimate, assume the characteristics of their creators. Men create and destroy values with equal intensity. As the only creature of historical memory, man reveres the past and yet ignores or denies it in the name of an utterly unknowable future.

More than 60 per cent of India's population lives in villages and most of them are devoid of even basic amenities. They toil to feed the rest of the nation with no viable means to better their lives. The schemes meticulously worked out by high-level committees to improve their lot invariably remain on paper. These simple folk accept hardship as their destiny. The contentment resulting from this bent of mind brings forth unfettered talent in multifaceted forms of folk-art. But what has gone unnoticed are the exotic forms that emerge from the use of basic materials at hand and the natural urge to create beauty in their habitat. Regardless of the type of building material, mud, wood, thatch or stone—each dwelling has an individuality and is in harmony with the environment. The villages are living galleries of unmatched forms comparable to any great work of art.

Our old cities and villages can inspire anyone in quest of new forms in the realm of architecture and planning. Corbusier admired the mud villages while Matthew Nowicki was deeply impressed by Rajasthani culture and indigenous architecture. This is clearly reflected in the plans and sketches Nowicki made for Chandigarh, which are on display in the City-Museum.

These breathtaking works of indigenous spontaneous art and architecture are on the decline and, with it, we are losing an aspect of our national heritage. With the passage of time, the influences of the overcrowded and polluted cities have resulted in the degeneration of folk-art and the disappearance of creative skills that manifest in vernacular architecture.

It was apparent even by the 1960s that this vernacular architecture was in decline. Over the years, I had become more and more interested in this subject. The geometric, masculine shapes of the Punjabi villages of my childhood were worth documenting. In 1965, soon after becoming the Chief Architect, I used up my modest savings, hired a photographer, and took leave for two months to visit villages in India, including the hilly regions and plains of Punjab and Haryana. I also visited the deserts of Rajasthan and the coastal region of India. I was never a good photographer, but I had a clear idea about the photographs I wanted. At the end of my travels, I had some amazing photographs that I hoped to compile into a book some day. I have guarded the photos carefully through the years, but have not found the time to write the book.

India could take heed from places elsewhere that have protected vernacular architecture. For example, in Santa Fe—the capital of New Mexico (U.S.A) houses similar to our village dwellings in form and texture exist. No buildings old or new are permitted to alter the existing style of architecture that is considered part of New Mexico's heritage. Similarly the physical character of our villages should not have been allowed to deteriorate under the influence of urban trends of architecture not suited to our rural setting. New building materials could have been used to complement the existing style and texture of mud dwellings. Satisfactory sanitation, essential health facilities and opportunities for job-related higher education must be made available in every village. Village populations should not be allowed to dwindle and avenues of adequate employment are imperative to stem the influx of rural youth to the overcrowded cities in search of livelihood. The monotonous blows of woodcutters' axe or carpenter's mallet, the merry voices of naked little children at play, the plaintive tune of ryot's song, the murmuring of leaves and singing birds all combine like moving strains of a grand dream—orchestra. The flow of village life is neither rapid nor stagnant. Work and rest go hand in hand. The exquisite combination of utilitarian forms and spontaneous art manifests in visual delight.

My brief visit from Shimla to see the new team of architects was not of much consequence, given the presence of the Chief Engineer and other, more senior officials. It was not until Le Corbusier's second visit that I began to know him. By then, we were working in Chandigarh in the temporary architect's office. The government had hired a number of additional Indian architects and planners from the Delhi School of Architecture and Planning. We all eagerly waited for the arrival of Corbusier in the only jeep available to the Architects's Office. Some of us gathered in a colleague's room, next to the porch and the parking lot from where we could have a clear view of the Master's arrival. It was exhilarating to watch the world's greatest architect stepping on the Chandigarh soil and we were excited at the opportunity to work with him. Before designing any building Le Corbusier viewed the site to realize the relationship of the building to its particular setting. Perhaps, the scale and form was as important to him as the functions of the building. Le Corbusier expressed his statements in diverse materials distinctively his own, innovative, dynamic and having a timeless quality. However hard we may have tried, it was difficult not to be inspired or influenced by the works of the great Master.

We revered Le Corbusier and observed him closely. His time was divided between work and work. He had no time to waste and every minute was precious. He never uttered a word without deep meaning or drew a line without great significance. He was a very hard task master and yet very kind and considerate to his associates.

Large numbers of drawings and the model of the High Court were displayed in the hall of the Chief Engineer's office in 1952 for Prime Minister Pandit Jawaharlal Nehru and the Judges of the High Court.

The design was explained in broad terms without delving much into the aspects of aesthetics. After about 45 minutes of viewing the exhibits Pandit Nehru showed his appreciation and gave his approval on the spot. Le Corbusier, by this great gesture of Panditji crossed the first hurdle to embark upon the other monumental edifices that now comprise the Capitol Complex.

Le Corbusier never explained his paintings or the aesthetics of his architectural creations or drawings, leaving it to the viewer to interpret. He once wrote 'For a finished and successful work holds within it, vast amount of intention, a variable world, which reveals itself to those who have a right to it: that is to say, to those who deserve it.'

Le Corbusier was way ahead of his time with his feet firmly rooted in past culture and its true values depicted in great works of art and architecture. He learnt from history and in turn made the architectural history rich and inspiring. One feels an abundance of diversity from different angles and contrasting perspectives. The Legislative Assembly may be one of the best examples. Space, light and volumes are always there as basic elements in Le Corbusier's creations. He remains a great sculptor in his paintings as well as in architecture.

The other architects and planners who assisted the Chandigarh Project were A.R. Prabhawalkar, Eulie Chaudhary, B.P. Mathur, Aditya Prakash, N.S Lamba, J.S. Dethe and Piloo Modi. All the architects were qualified from overseas universities except for B.P. Mathur and J.S. Dethe. They were supported by Assistant Architects, including Jeet Malhotra. Some of these architects also worked for Le Corbusier meritoriously.

Giani Rattan Singh deserves special mention as the most versatile in assisting Le Corbusier by making accurate models of the buildings. He also helped me and other architects. In recognition of the meritorious service, I employed him even after his retirement until he was unable to work given his deteriorating eyesight. I also recommended his son to serve in his place.

At my request Corbusier was considerate enough to accompany me to visit my architectural works like Government Printing Press (Sector 18), Officer's Hostel (Sector 10) that was later altered and renamed Hotel Mount View, Central Police Station (Sector 17), Boys Polytechnic Campus (Sector 26) including my father's house (Sector 10) that was designed in 1955. It was a modest single-storey three-bedroom house. Its curved exposed front brick wall with its carefully designed opening and wide plastered sculptural jali in rubble stone wall fascinated Le Corbusier. He also admired the play of light and shadow. I also accompanied him to the Town Hall and the Central State Library in the City Centre for which I was associated with Pierre Jeanneret.

In the mornings, Le Corbusier used to go to the construction sites to see his buildings in progress. By nine or ten he arrived at the Architect's Office

Le Corbusier, Pierre Jeanneret,
M.N. Sharma, P.L. Varma at a
get together, 1956
Source: M.N. Sharma

to work on details for buildings under construction and for drawings sent from Paris. Indian architects assigned to assist Le Corbusier were called interns. In the afternoons, Le Corbusier and Jeanneret went home for lunch. While Jeanneret came back after lunch, Le Corbusier stayed back for his regular afternoon session of painting before returning to the office at about 4.30 p.m. Again he would start working with the interns on different drawings. On every visit Le Corbusier engraved a rubber stamp, which he used on every drawing he made in Chandigarh. There are 23 such stamps in the archives of the Fondation Le Corbusier in Paris.

Le Corbusier had no time for social engagements and remained busy during working hours. We seldom had any discussions with him as our

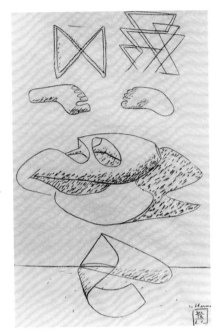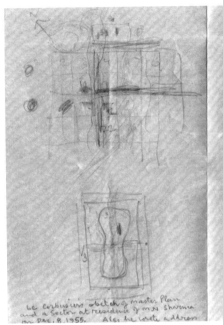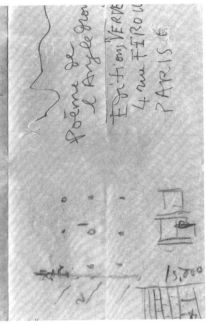

interactions remained mostly confined to work. However, my office was close to the men's washroom and Le Corbusier would usually pop his head into my office as he returned from there just to ask how things were progressing. One of our projects together was the unbuilt Post and Telecommunications Building, which was to be 11 storeys high, in the City Centre. During one of the work sessions, I wanted Le Corbusier to clarify certain aspect of the building design. He started talking on a different subject and after a little while, got back to solve my problem. It became evident that he took his time to give satisfactory answers. He could do both—think differently and talk at the same time. Corbusier light-heartedly joked at times.

Le Corbusier's inner self was revealed through his paintings and acts of kindness, more than spoken words. Once he mentioned that his pet dog, being very old and sick, had to be put to sleep. He described how he took the pet to the veterinary surgeon for the last act with a very heavy heart. The dog trustingly put his head in Le Corbusier's hands and was put to sleep.

Nothing escaped Le Corbusier's notice. One day I was pleasantly surprised by his visit to my room where an apprentice architect from Afghanistan was sitting opposite me and drawing a jug. Le Corbusier looked at the

Above left:
A sketch by Le Corbusier, gifted to M.N. Sharma
Source: M.N. Sharma

Above right:
Le Corbusier drew a rough sketch of the master plan and a sector, during an informal visit to M.N. Sharma's residence, December 1955;
Source: M.N. Sharma

figure, corrected it and walked away with a smile. On another day, during our work-session, Le Corbusier observed a bull in the office-lawns. He quickly walked out, took the sketch book and a pen from his safari-jacket and drew a beautiful sketch of the bull which was later published.

Le Corbusier believed in simplicity in living and very high ideals of life. Yet, he was careful with his dress and was always spotlessly attired in a comfortable safari suit for work, and most immaculately dressed for formal occasions. Le Corbusier was very sympathetic towards hard-working persons and even animals. He was very impressed by the load-carrying donkeys and often compared himself with their lot. It made me wonder if he would consider making a statue of a donkey at an important location as a tribute to the humble animal that worked so hard in the making of Chandigarh during the time when not many machines were used. Almost everything in the city was made by hand by labourers from other states, who carried loads of building materials on their heads over temporary wooden scaffolding, climbing as high as the buildings. It looked like a very dangerous working situation, but I do not remember any casualty at the work site.

Contrary to the general perception, Le Corbusier was always receptive to the ideas of others, especially regarding a building's functioning. I recall that after the High Court was built, lawyers and their clients complained about the lack of protection from the summer sun and heavy rains while walking to the courtrooms. I wondered what Le Corbusier would do to the monumental building. He made a wide veranda in front of the courtrooms without affecting the main building. One hardly notices the thin concrete roof of the veranda or the slender steel columns. Similarly he added many more court rooms with recessed brick-walls without affecting the main High Court Facade. Le Corbusier appreciated and readily agreed with P.L. Varma to build a dam at the Sukhna Choe to form the Sukhana Lake. This allowed him to make a three kilometer-wide boulevard dedicated to citizens to get away from the humdrum city life and enjoy nature in tranquility.

Le Corbusier personally knew me as he had visited my buildings with me and on his own. I often met him in the office and he even visited my house several times. Some of the architects, including myself, also met Le Corbusier for evening get togethers at Pierre Jeanneret's house in

Sector 5. In late 1958 I was asked to assist Le Corbusier on two projects—the Post and Telegraph Office building in Sector-17 and the Sports Stadium for 50,000 spectators and Sports Village towards the eastern side of Sukhna Lake. For these projects of Le Corbusier, drawings of the buildings were sent from Paris in metric scale for further work. I was given the sketch designs of the aforementioned two buildings to be developed under his personal supervision and further instructions. Regarding the 11-storeyed Post and Telegraph building I was told to draw the basic plan, its typical sections and façades and to assess the volumetric appearance in relation to its surroundings. Before dealing with the monumental manifestation of his works, he wanted to ensure that, there were breaks in the structure to relieve the monotony and he was concerned with the size of the vertical louvres which offered some protection during the different periods of the year. In fact, he was seeking perfection in the basic unit of the façade. I began to understand the logic of Le Corbusier's design process and the manner in which he crafted his monumental works.

Interior of Pierre Jeanneret's house in Sector 5, Chandigarh
Source: M.N. Sharma

Facing page:
A sketch sent to M.N. Sharma by Le Corbusier in 1957 on Yvonne Le Corbusier's death
Source: M.N. Sharma

During an important meeting with the top officials of the Post and Telegraph Offices, the officials were of the view that they did not need an 11-storey building. I suggested to Le Corbusier that we agree to a four-storey structure to begin with and add foundations strong enough for an eventual 11-storeys. My suggestion was based on the assumption that by the time four storeys had been constructed, there would be a demand for more offices. Le Corbusier agreed to consider my suggestion. However, on his way to back to Paris, he discussed the matter with P.L. Varma in Delhi who urged him to insist on the 11-storey building. This was not accepted; the site has remained vacant ever since, and the most important plaza of the city has never been completed.

The 11-storey building, by virtue of its location near the Town Hall (Estate Office) and visible from all sides in the city centre, would have been the most prestigious building in the entire city. This would have given

Chandigarh, another landmark to its inventory of Le Corbusier buildings and would have added to the tourist attractions of Chandigarh.

I continued working with Le Corbusier for over four years. Time did not permit us to continue because I was selected to take care of the projects for Punjab State, as I was transferred to Patiala in December 1962. All the drawings were left in the cupboard of my office room in

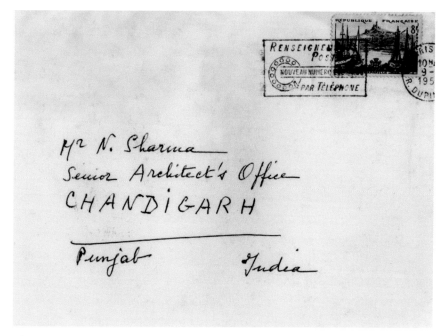

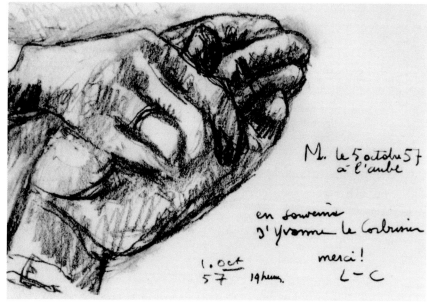

Chandigarh. Unfortunately these drawings have not been located. The projects were never designed further and remain unimplemented. I often visited Chandigarh for official meetings to meet Le Corbusier during the years 1962–1965 to discuss architecture with him.

Le Corbusier was very generous to me. He recognized my single-minded focus on architecture and talent. In appreciation of my works that he had seen, he gifted me a beautiful big sketch done by him in 1956. I was again deeply touched by Corbusier's affection when I received a card announcing his wife Yvonne Corbusier's death on 5th October 1957. It was a beautiful sketch of two hands holding each other, that he sent to very close friends. It was much later I came to know that I was the only Indian architect to receive this sketch.

A few times, I invited Le Corbusier to my place for drinks. These occasions gave me the opportunity to discuss architecture as well as to show respect to him. During one of his visits, my son Manu who was four years old came close to Le Corbusier to seek his attention. Le Corbusier lovingly spoke to him in simple English and gave him a small shell from his pocket. Manu still has this shell as his most precious possession.

In one very high-level and meeting concerning the 11-storey Post and Telegraph Building in our office, I casually mentioned to Le Corbusier that I had to catch a bus to go to Delhi. During the meeting Le Corbusier reminded me twice to leave the meeting in order to avoid delay to go to Delhi. I deeply appreciated his concern for me.

Le Corbusier paid attention to people close to him and helped whenever possible. Once during an informal discussion in my house, I sought some clarification about the master plan and the 11-storey Post and Telegraph building in Sector 17. While Le Corbusier was drawing it at the back of a letter from my father, I also asked him where I could get his latest publication 'Poem of the Right Angle'. He immediately wrote the address of the Publisher on one corner of same letter responding to my request. A photocopy of this letter with Le Corbusier's sketch and publisher's address is displayed in the Le Corbusier Centre in Sector 19.

Le Corbusier was very judicious and precise in his letters to Pandit Jawaharlal Nehru regarding his works and major violations in the periphery. He never interfered in the administrative matters and remained confined to his works.

Le Corbusier rarely expressed his attitude towards religion as spiritual modesty restrained him. That is why one listened with even greater attention when he broke the silence. In an interview he replied,

> I have made churches Ronchamp and La Tourette. That elicited an undoubtedly religious emotion. I am not myself a practicing Christian, but one thing I know that every man has the religious feeling in being part of a human wealth. To a greater or a lesser degree, it will always be part of it. In my work I feel such profuse emotion and intense inner life that it almost becomes religious. It is not to be proclaimed with the drums beating.

I often wondered if Le Corbusier believed in God and I came to know the truth from his last write-up in July 1965. It appears like his last testament. I like to quote that in parts. Le Corbusier writes,

> ...Every thing that one learns in the schools, in the political clubs, at the dancing lessons, amount to a constellation of fixed points of each individual, an unalterable design, a defensive barrier between the free judgment and the free and proper use of things given us by God Almighty or the arrangements thereof offered by other men...

Le Corbusier also revealed his belief in the existence of soul as the true self of any living being in his spontaneous parting remark to his former assistant Tobito who expressed his wish to visit him again '...Here or on another planet', which proved prophetic as Le Corbusier suddenly died a month later on 27 August 1965.

While Le Corbusier showed appreciation for good deeds, he did not forget any injustice done to him. He spoke of not getting the due credit for the design of the U.N. Building in New York which was very similar to the proposals made by him when he was invited along with few other selected architects to propose designs. Le Corbusier was also resentful that his design for the Palace of Soviets in Moscow in 1934, which had earlier drawn a lot of attention had not been accepted. He declined to go there when invited by the Prime Minister of U.S.S.R. Nikolai Alexandrovich

Bulganin and the First Secretary of the Communist Party, during their visit to his office in Chandigarh in November 1955.

Many heads of nations visited Chandigarh to marvel at the new concept of the city and his great edifices for the Capitol Complex. In addition to Marshal Tito of Yugoslavia, I remember the visit of the President of Brazil Jusceilino Kubitschek and his team at the time Brazilia was being designed. India offered Le Corbusier not only the largest commission of his life but also the immense richness of an old and complex civilization.

Le Corbusier deeply appreciated Indian culture and in return, he gave visual expression to most of his beliefs and ideology that established the Modern Movement of Architecture on Indian soil. Le Corbusier expressed his wish in the last write up in July 1965 beseeching his friend Andre Malraux, Minister of Culture in France, to help in the implementation of the Open Hand in Chandigarh. I have great satisfaction that I was able to fulfil Le Corbusier's most cherished wish by getting the Open Hand made and installed in the Capitol Complex, before accepting the assignment of the Consultant Advisor for the New Federal Capital of Nigeria in 1979.

After returning to Chandigarh in the year 1997, I have been making sincere endeavors for creating awareness among the citizens and the authorities for the genuine causes of the city through media and personal contacts. In doing so, I am fulfilling the wishes of the Master who enshrined history with his most magnificent edifices that made him the greatest architect of the 20th century.

Excerpted from: *Making of Chandigarh: Le Corbusier and After* by M.N. Sharma.

Courtesy: M.N. Sharma Architectural Society, Chandigarh.

ENDNOTES

COMMEMORATING LE CORBUSIER'S LEGACY

50 years after the master

July–October 2015

Rajnish Wattas

Deepika Gandhi

Celebrating
Le Corbusier's Chandigarh

The 50th death anniversary of Le Corbusier falling on 27th August 2015 was commemorated in architectural circles all over the world, especially the academia as a landmark day. Various events such as symposiums, design competitions, exhibitions, etc., were held discussing, debating and showcasing his contribution to the evolution of Modern architecture globally. The city of Chandigarh—his greatest realisation, too, most enthusiastically and befittingly, commemorated the special year on an unprecedented scale. A series of lectures, seminars and related events, celebrating his creative genius and contribution to the city in particular and to world architecture at large, were organised.

An extended series of activities started in July 2015 itself, as a build-up to the actual day of his 50th Death Anniversary falling on 27th August 2015. The nearly four-months-long commemoration culminated with celebrations to mark his birth anniversary on 6th October 1987 as well as Chandigarh's official inauguration on 7th October 1953.

The target audience of these mega-events was not confined to the architectural fraternity alone, but encompassed all the citizens of Chandigarh to sensitise them towards the uniqueness of their modern heritage and why it needed to be protected. To fulfil this objective a series of basic lectures were held for students and teachers of various schools and colleges in the city regarding the architecture, planning and unique features of Chandigarh, as the first planned city of modern India. A booklet titled *Chandigarh—My City Beautiful* outlining the creation and critical components of the city was also launched that now forms a part of the non-graded curriculum of all government schools in the city. Conducted tours and audio-visual lectures were held at the Chandigarh Architecture Museum and at the Le Corbusier Centre of the city, its two main architectural history centres. The sustained interest and involvement of the residents in these celebrations was facilitated by holding of popular events like 'Treasure Hunts' and 'On-the-spot painting competitions' held at key heritage points of the city on offbeat, imaginative themes based on the various facets of the Capitol Complex and the city as a whole. On similar lines, photography and design competitions were floated for citizens and architectural colleges encompassing the city and the adjoining regions, impelling people to look at the city and its spaces from a different perspective, which evoked tremendous response.

A unique initiative, *'Chandigarh Samvaad'*—a series of expert-citizen interactions promoted by the Chandigarh Administration in collaboration with a major national newspaper, was launched to enable an open dialogue and interface between the city administration, key stakeholders and the citizens of Chandigarh on the various challenges facing the city in critical areas like traffic and transport, health, education, etc. The sessions were conducted in popular public places like the Open Hand plaza in the Capitol Complex, City Centre Sector 17 plaza and the Leisure Valley, along with venues in the Southern Sectors of the city also, which house the maximum density of residents. These sessions drew a very enthusiastic response from the citizens and threw up many issues that were duly noted by the representatives of the Administration for follow-up—and actually implemented later.

However, the biggest achievement of the four-month-long celebrations was perhaps the opening up of the Capitol Complex to the citizens of Chandigarh for easy entry (earlier restricted by cumbersome security permissions). This hugely important step—both physical and symbolic—was carried forward by hosting a series of events, aesthetic illumination at night and launch of conducted tours of the Capitol Complex. The wide coverage by the local and national media ensured that the connection between the citizens and their city was restored and strengthened, accomplishing a prime objective of all the celebrations and events.

The grand finale of this long series of activities was the International Symposium 'Celebrating Le Corbusier's Chandigarh' held from 9 to 12 October 2015. The symposium provided a platform for eminent global architects, urban planners and historians to discuss and debate the legacy of Le Corbusier as manifested in the city of Chandigarh and beyond, world over—with special focus on the Capitol Complex and the city.

The colloquium not limited to being an academic exercise alone, also provided a forum for the Chandigarh Administration to seek advice from the experts regarding the multiple challenges and issues that the city faces today in conserving its precious modern architectural heritage on the one hand and balancing the same with the city's burgeoning growth as a vibrant, Smart city on the other. The symposium saw an enthusiastic response from architects, students and scholars with over a thousand registrations. The venue of the Symposium, the Tagore Theatre—a landmark symbol of Chandigarh's early growth period, was abuzz with activity, a photo exhibition, stalls by reputed publishers, manufacturers and retailers of architectural products and local NGOs. All the sessions witnessed a packed hall with very few people availing the free conducted tours of the city offered—perhaps a testimony to the engaging presentations and enlightening panel discussions that followed each session!

Coinciding with the Symposium, the Embassy of Switzerland in India organized an exhibition titled 'Le Corbusier—Mastering the Image' from 10 to 23 October 2015 as a part of the 'Year of Swiss Innovation in India'. The exhibition focussing on Corbusier's relationship with photography showcased over 150 images, many having been taken by Corbusier himself and exhibited in Chandigarh for the first time.

The symposium and the events leading up to it rejuvenated the long ignored connect between the city and its various stake holders. The deliberations and debates provided the Administration with some much needed indicators to the future course of action, while preparing for the World Heritage nomination of the Capitol Complex, which finally got accepted and inscribed by UNESCO in July 2016.

Even as the four-month-long enthusiastic commemoration of Le Corbusier's 50th death anniversary was a huge success in achieving the

Facing page above:
The book *Le Corbusier: Idea and Form* by William J.R. Curtis being released by then Governor of Punjab during the inaugural ceremony of the symposium.
Photo courtesy:
Chandigarh College of Architecture, Chandigarh

Facing page below:
The symposium provided a platform for discussions and debates on the future course of Chandigarh.
Photo courtesy:
Chandigarh College of Architecture, Chandigarh

Pp. 228–29:
Geometric hill in Capitol Complex, Chandigarh
© Rajiv Kumar

goals set out—yet a lot still needs to be done to engage the citizens at every level with their urban heritage. Fortunately awareness is rising as the outreach and education programs—especially for students and teachers are ongoing.

Finally, the citizens are beginning to 'own' their City and its multi-faceted heritage.

CAPITOL COMPLEX
Road to UNESCO

Rajnish Wattas
Deepika Gandhi

The Capitol Complex in Chandigarh is one of the most monumental architectural compositions of Modern urbanism by Le Corbusier—an important part of his global legacy, arising out of a unique geo-political and cultural setting. It showcases landmark innovations in the fields of urban planning, architectural theory and practice as well as advancement in building materials and technology. Hence, though, not surprising but still a matter of great pride for Chandigarh and India at large is the honour bestowed on the Capitol Complex as a part of the 'Transnational Nomination of Architectural and Urban Planning works of Le Corbusier' for the World Heritage List 2016 along with six other state parties.

This nomination consisting of a subset of 17 buildings belonging to the architectural work of Le Corbusier is the result of a joint undertaking initiated more than 10 years ago by the Fondation Le Corbusier, Paris along with seven other countries. The numerous critical works of Corbusier located in Germany, Argentina, Belgium, France, India, Japan and Switzerland, form a cohesive group showcasing the multi-faceted influence of Le Corbusier's work on a worldwide level. The nomination of these properties under the 'Cultural Serial' Category fulfilled the following criteria as listed in the UNESCO world heritage guidelines:

Criteria (ii): Exhibit an important interchange of human values, over a span of time or within a cultural area of the world, on developments

Facing page:
High Court in Capitol
Complex, Chandigarh
© Rajiv Kumar

Pp: 230–31
Assembly building,
Tower of Shadows
in Capitol Complex,
Chandigarh
© Rajiv Kumar

in architecture or technology, monumental arts, town-planning or landscape design.

Criteria (vi): Be directly or tangibly associated with events or living traditions, with ideas, or with beliefs, with artistic and literary works of outstanding universal significance.

Criteria (i): 'To be a work of human genius', was added later during the nomination process underway in Istanbul in July 2016. The addition of this criterion seems befitting as this ensemble of monuments and edifices of the Complex represents the most tangible manifestation of the architectural and urban design theories of Le Corbusier. The unprecedented amalgamation of the principles of CIAM (Congrès International d'Architecture Moderne), with the aspirations of the newly created democracy culminated in a creation which continues to deeply impact the development of architecture and urban planning all over the world. Considered as his most mature plastic creations, each of the edifices and monuments has a unique sculptural form based on its function and a strong symbolism inherent in the form derived for each building. Here one sees a tangible manifestation of the principles of Purism and Brutalism uniquely tempered by the use of colours to offset the monochromatic finish of the exposed concrete. The extensive use of *brise-soleil* and double roofs for solar control, orientation and design of fenestrations for trans-aeration, reflecting pools for rain water harvesting and thermal sinks, terrace gardens etc., were technological innovations for climate responsive architecture. The creation of complex forms based on a simple structural order within the limited resources of time, money and manpower was a landmark in the advancement of architectural techniques in Chandigarh, India and the world at large.

The nomination process of the Capitol Complex started way back in 2014 with the Ministry of Culture, Government of India, approving inclusion of the Capitol Complex in the Transnational Serial nomination of Le Corbusier's work that was being coordinated by the Fondation Le Corbusier, Paris. The Dossier and detailed Management plan for the property had been prepared and submitted to the Fondation in July 2014. An expert from International Council on Monuments and Sites (ICOMOS) visited the Capitol Complex in October 2015 to review the ground situation of the site and the state of implementation of measures outlined in the

Facing page:
Assembly building—before and after cleaning and restoration
© Rajiv Kumar

management plan. The report of the expert was overall very positive and the reply to some clarifications sought by ICOMOS was sent in February 2016. Further clarifications to ICOMOS, mainly regarding the buffer area towards the Shivalik hills, have been dealt by the Administration from time to time through the Fondation. A standing subcommittee of Chandigarh Heritage Conservation Committee has been formed by the Chandigarh Administration to periodically review the implementation of the Management Plan and to streamline execution of the commitments made by the Administration.

To ensure cooperation and cohesion in the management of the entire nomination, an International Standing Conference between the seven state parties has been set up by the Fondation. The prerogatives of each country in terms of protection, conservation and heritage management for their individual sites are given due regard within this purview. In February 2016, a meeting of all state parties that are part of the Standing Conference was held in Chandigarh with subsequent meetings held at the Fondation's office in Paris to chalk out the future course of action.

A critical component for the nomination that enabled success in its acceptance was the authenticity and integrity of the Capitol Complex which is well maintained in the realised components as well as in its general layout. Since the Complex falls under Grade 1 heritage zone of Chandigarh, no major structural or planning changes that can have a discernible impact on the authenticity have been allowed. Also, there are several certified documents relating to the conception, creation, execution and development of the Capitol and its components to establish the degree of authenticity.

THE MANAGEMENT PLAN FOR THE CAPITOL COMPLEX

An important concern of ICOMOS while considering a property for inscription on the World Heritage list is the robustness of the mechanism to safeguard the 'Outstanding Universal Values (OUVs)' in the future. The management plan for the Capitol was thus formulated with utmost care to cover every aspect possible. A detailed assessment of the present condition of the site and its components formed the basis for the management plan in the dossier for the Capitol. The current usage and management of the site, the needs of its stakeholders, present means of protection and legislation, visitor management, risk preparedness measures and current state of the structures were studied in detail. Data was collected from different sources to identify number of employees and visitors, list of additions and alterations undertaken in the buildings over the years, maintenance staff and procedures, reports of fire audits and risk assessment, etc. This database was then analysed in relation to the OUVs of the site to identify the issues and challenges that could pose a threat to the OUV or dilute the authenticity and integrity of the site.

These identified issues were then formulated into future tasks and monitoring indices for the systematic implementation of the management plan. Timelines were assigned to each monitoring index based on past precedence, complexity of work, number of agencies involved and the urgency of the task being considered. All this data was tabulated clearly indicating the task, tentative timeline and agency or department responsible for its implementation.

CHALLENGES TO THE SITE

The Capitol Complex, has been approved as a Grade 1 heritage precinct by the Government of India on the recommendation of the Expert Heritage Committee constituted by it and thus enjoys protection at the highest level. However, the greatest challenge for the conservation of the Capitol Complex is that it is a 'living heritage site' and being extensively used as the administrative head of the city by the states of Punjab and Haryana. The maintenance and conservation of the exposed concrete of the edifices, monuments and plaza is another challenge as it is one of the critical OUVs of the complex. This is being addressed in a holistic manner to address both structural and aesthetic concerns.

Within the buildings, the challenges are compounded by the diverse needs of multiple stake holders, an increasing pressure on space usage; need to introduce modern amenities and continuously evolving spatial and functional requirements. The largest section of stakeholders comprises of the nearly 12,000 employees working in all the three buildings. The Chief Ministers of Punjab and Haryana and other senior officers also have their offices in the Secretariat building, necessitating rigorous security measures. There are many visitors who come for purely official work to

the Secretariat building while around 5,000 litigants and advocates visit the High Court daily besides the judges.

At the site level, balancing tourist access with security concerns and the escalating need for parking are the main challenges. Due to the sensitive functions of all the buildings the Complex requires high security for which various security agencies have close to 1,300 security personnel deputed in and around the nominated property. Since they are responsible for round the clock security of the Complex their accommodation and allied services need to be catered to as close to the core areas as possible presenting an aesthetic and functional dilemma.

At the urban level the precincts of the nominated property fall under the Chandigarh Administration and are thus well protected under existing legislation as Heritage Grade 1. The backdrop of the Shivalik range is vital to the integrity of the layout as it was the very basis for the layout

17 July 2016 : Successful inscripton of the trans-national dossier to the UNESCO World Heritage Status at the Istanbul meet. Photo courtesy : Kapil Setia

of the Complex. However, preserving this vista poses a great challenge and is being addressed through inter-state dialogue as the area falls under Punjab.

Even before starting the nomination process Chandigarh's Department of Urban Planning identified the areas requiring immediate attention for protecting the OUVs of the property such as the conservation of the built fabric of the edifices, monuments and plaza, completing the original composition and landscape design of the site and preserving the views and vistas. Pedestrian continuity had to be restored as per the original layout. To facilitate user, tourist and visitor management, infrastructural augmentation of the property has been undertaken to address developmental pressures and increased visitation while ensuring the preservation of the authenticity and integrity of the site and its components. The increasing pressure on parking for the High Court and Secretariat buildings has been catered to by provision of additional parking in areas that do not compromise the layout and scale of the open spaces critical to the nominated site.

A risk management plan to counter all possible hazards such as fire, disaster and emergency situations in and around the nominated property is being formulated to safeguard the buildings and their users. The integration of educational and outreach programmes has been geared towards sensitising the visitors, users and stakeholders regarding the heritage of the property. A comprehensive interpretation plan has been developed through various interpretive mediums including signage, publications, brochures and a dedicated website for the Capitol Complex.

However, it was not enough to merely frame rules and policies in the management plan as they need to be diligently implemented and closely monitored. The indicators for monitoring the site are the factors that protect the authenticity and integrity of the site and thus measure the success or weakness of the Management Plan. The indicators were tabulated for monitoring, frequency of monitoring and the authority responsible for the same. As stated before the Capitol Complex is a living heritage and constantly under developmental, environmental and political pressures—some of which cannot be anticipated at the time of finalising the Management Plan. Developments in the future and emergence of new areas of concern may necessitate revisiting certain policies and creation of new ones to address the changed realities. To address both the scenarios the Management Plan shall thus be reviewed in 2020.

The Chandigarh Administration is completely committed to the implementation of the Management Plan for the protection and conservation of the Capitol Complex and is undertaking on high priority the measures necessary for the successful completion of all targets and monitoring indices in a time-bound manner. The most tangible manifestation of this commitment has been the massive exercise undertaken for the sprucing up of the entire site and its vital components since 2014.

The Capitol Complex was conceived by Le Corbusier as a symbol of democracy and he thus envisaged it as a grand public space buzzing with activity. However, due to security concerns the entire premises was made off limits for citizens with very limited access to tourists and visitors as well. Heavy security and barricading of the pedestrian plaza

Facing page:
Capitol Complex—before and after cleaning and restoration
© Rajiv Kumar

also marred the beauty of the Complex compromising on the most critical tenet of Corbusier's layout. Low visitation and barricading lead to further decay of the ensemble due to minimal maintenance of the plaza and the building facades. Unchecked growth of random plantation and trees obscured the vistas and views so carefully planned by Corbusier. To resolve these issues deliberations were held between the Chandigarh Administration, the security and maintenance agencies and other stake holders to work out a time bound plan for the sprucing up of the Complex and to facilitate access and visitation. The barricade dividing the plaza was finally removed in 2015 to allow free access from the High court to the Assembly building thus restoring the essence of the space.

A massive operation for cleaning, repairing and relaying of the concrete floor of the plaza was undertaken and successfully completed in 2015. The pathways and connections between the Monuments and buildings were completed as per the original scheme. The Department of Urban Planning undertook a detailed mapping of the existing plants and trees on site and after many visits on site to assess their impact on the vistas, a scheme was prepared, clearly marking the plantation and trees to be removed or pruned to clear the visual clutter that had ensued due to years of neglect. The grand plaza is now a sight to behold and does full justice as the foreground for the most iconic creations of Le Corbusier. The concrete of the façades of all the three buildings has been cleaned as per the guidelines of the Central Building Research Institute, Roorkee which has also submitted a report on the complete structural and seismic assessment of the Secretariat building and recommendations for the future course of action. The majestic sight of the completed Geometric hill with the 24-hour cycle mural on its concrete slope flanked by the spruced up Tower of Shadows and Martyr's Memorial have made the long walk across the plaza a powerful visual experience indeed.

CONSOLIDATING HERITAGE AND TOURISM

To facilitate tourists and visitors a Tourist Information Centre at the entry to the Complex from the Jan Marg was inaugurated in 2014 to provide information and permission for visiting the Capitol Complex. The three guided tours every day have received a good response and substantially increased visitation as permission can now easily be obtained online from the website of the Department of Tourism.

Governor, Sh. V.P. Singh
Badnore at the inauguration
of Maison Jeanneret Museum,
Sector 5, Chandigarh
Photo courtesy: Le Corbusier
Centre, Chandigarh

The visitors to the Capitol are increasing not just quantitatively but qualitatively as well! The visit of the then President of France, Mr Francois Hollande and the Indian Prime Minister, Mr Narendra Modi, on 24th January 2016 was a historic moment for the Capitol Complex and Chandigarh—as it brought this magnificent architectural ensemble into international limelight. It was a much-needed endorsement of the universal value of the Capitol Complex. Perhaps impressed by the grandeur of the Capitol plaza, the Prime Minister personally chose it as the venue for the celebration of the International Yoga Day on 21st June 2016, which he led himself. Thousands of people attended the event, once again bringing the Capitol to international attention and most importantly acknowledging it as an important part of our Indian Heritage.

Pierre Jeanneret, Le Corbusier's cousin and almost lifelong work associate, has contributed to the urban morphology and architectural character of Chandigarh as deeply and widely as Corbusier. From 1951 to 1965 Jeanneret was the anchor of the creation and development of Chandigarh

and he stayed on as the Chief Architect of Chandigarh from 1955–65 with his legacy continuing to impact the city till date. The house designed by Jeanneret where he lived for almost 11 years had lost much of its original fabric and concept due to frequent additions and alterations over the years. As a befitting tribute to both the house and its creator, the Chandigarh Administration decided to restore the house and establish a museum dedicated to the life and works of Jeanneret. Deepika Gandhi, Director, Le Corbusier Centre and Chandigarh Architecture Museum supervised the painstaking repair and restoration of the house and curated the Jeanneret Museum which was inaugurated on 22nd March 2017 by His Excellency Sh. V.P. Singh Badnore, Governor Punjab & Administrator UT Chandigarh.

The Government Museum and Art Gallery designed by Corbusier on his concept of 'museum of unlimited growth' will complete 50 years of its establishment this year. This well-preserved building with its priceless

Open Hand in Capitol Complex, Chandigarh
Photo courtesy:
Chandigarh tourism

Pp. 248–49
Drone view of Capitol Complex, Chandigarh
Photo courtesy:
Chandigarh tourism

collection is being modernised with audio guides, a robust outreach and education program and an increased social media presence. The Chandigarh Architecture Museum has also launched a series of guided tours for school students with special sensitisation workshops being held for school educators on a regular basis.

The green cover and landscape of Chandigarh is as much a part of its urban fabric and architectural legacy as its built environment. Chandigarh Tree lovers (CTL)—a citizens' initiative supported by Times of India group, was recently launched to celebrate and protect the trees of Chandigarh and has been evoking passionate support from citizens of varied age groups and professions.

These heartening developments show that even as Chandigarh gears towards becoming a Smart City it is very much aware of its immense architectural heritage. The Chandigarh Administration ably supported by the proud citizens of the city are committed to take all measures to celebrate and cherish not just the Capitol Complex but the entire city of Chandigarh.

CONTRIBUTORS

Alfredo Brillembourg

Alfredo Brillembourg received his Bachelor of Art and Architecture in 1984 and his Master of Science in Architectural Design in 1986 from Columbia University. In 1992, he received a second architecture degree from the Central University of Venezuela and began his independent practice in architecture. In 1993 he founded Urban-Think Tank (U-TT) in Caracas, Venezuela. Starting in 2007, Brillembourg has been a guest professor at the Graduate School of Architecture and Planning, Columbia University, where he co-founded the Sustainable Living Urban Model Laboratory.

Brillembourg holds the chair for Architecture and Urban Design at the Swiss Institute of Technology (Eidgenossische Technische Hochschule, ETH) in Zurich, Switzerland. As co-principle of U-TT, he received the 2010 Ralph Erskine Award, the 2011 Holcim Gold Award for Latin America, the 2012 Holcim Global Silver Award for innovative contributions to ecological design practices and the 2012 Golden Lion Award in the 13th Venice Architecture Biennale.

Balkrishna V. Doshi

Dr Balkrishna V. Doshi is a Fellow of Royal Institute of British Architects as well as The Indian Institute of Architects. He worked with Le Corbusier from 1951 to 1957.

He has been a jury member for several international and national awards including The Aga Khan Award and the Pritzker Prize and held important chairs.

He is nationally and internationally known as an educator and institution builder. He has received many national and international awards and honarary Doctorates from University of Pennsylvania and McGill University and was awarded as an Officer of the order of Arts and Letters, by the Government of France.

Balkrishna Doshi is foremost among the modern Indian architects and has to his credit outstanding projects ranging from dozens of townships to several educational campuses, which include those for CEPT University Ahmedabad, NIFT New Delhi and IIM Bangalore.

Deepika Gandhi

An alumnus and faculty of the Chandigarh College of Architecture since 2002, she is presently holding the charge of Director Le Corbusier Centre & Chandigarh Architecture Museum. She was the Secretary Symposium for the International Symposium Celebrating Le Corbusier's Chandigarh on which this publication is based.

Having worked on the preparation of the Dossier for the world heritage nomination of the Capitol Complex she has since been engaged in promoting the heritage of Chandigarh at all levels.

She supervised the repair and restoration of the Pierre Jeanneret house and established the Jeanneret Museum there, while also restoring the Le Corbusier Centre.

She has co-authored the book *Sukhna—Sublime Lake of Chandigarh* and authored and designed booklets 'Chandigarh—My city beautiful' and 'Nek Chand's Rock Garden' to sensitise students about their heritage.

Jagan Shah

Jagan Shah is the Director of National Institute of Urban Affairs (NIUA), the premier think tank of the Ministry of Urban Development, Government of India. NIUA is the national Project Management Unit for the Heritage City Development and Angmentation Yojana Scheme for heritage cities. It is also the strategic partner and 'single window' for the capacity building programme to support the AMRUT Mission.

NIUA is deeply involved with the Smart City Mission. Shah has 20 years of professional work. He studied Architecture Design from the School of Planning and Architecture (SPA), New Delhi and Architectural History and Theory from the University of Cincinnati and Columbia University in New York.

Jacques Sbriglio

Jacques Sbriglio is a practising architect and urban planner based in the area of Marseilles. He is also a State Advisory Architect for the cities of Grenoble and Montpellier and teaches architectural theory and design at the Ecole Nationale Supérieure d'Architecture de Marseille-Luminy.

Jacques Sbriglio has published numerous works and produced several exhibitions on modern and contemporary architecture in Europe, Asia and South America about Le Corbusier's works. The last one was in Marseilles about the topic: Le Corbusier et la Question du Brutalism in 2013.

He has particularly focused on Le Corbusier's housing projects, devoting a series of monographs to key dwellings such as the La Roche and Jeanneret Houses, the Villa Savoye, the apartment block on rue Nungesser et Coli, and the unites d'habitation, built both in and outside France.

M.N. Sharma (1923–2016)

Born on 4 August 1923, M.N. Sharma joined the Capitol project in June 1950 and worked with the American team for the first master plan and in 1951 joined the team of the architects led by Le Corbusier. Sharma was chosen to be the first chief architect in 1965 after the retirement of Pierre Jeanneret.

Sharma recently wrote a book *Making of Chandigarh: Le Corbusier and After* which described the chronology of the events of the making of the city.

He was the recipient of many national and international awards for his contribution to the profession, including the award of the Institute of Life (France) for creating the best environment for the common man, in 1973. For his devotion to the profession the Chandigarh administration conferred the lifetime achievement award on him in October 2015.

Michel Richard

Born in 1947, Michel Richard has been the executive manager of the Fondation Le Corbusier in Paris since 2004. He studied literature at the University of Caen and has specalized in linguistics and in Irish and American literature. After a few years experience as an actor in a theatre company he joined the ministry of Culture where he holds several positions in the field of Cultural Development. He has held successive responsibilities related to reading policies and book programmes. Later on he has been in charge of the photographic and multimedia department of the National Museums organisation.

P.L. Varma (1901–1995)

P.L. Varma was born on 21 May 1901. In 1924 he passed with credit from Thompson Engineering College Roorkee. He was a brilliant engineer, who had a very distinguished career in the PWD (B&R) Punjab from 1924 to 1956. He was Chief Engineer & Secretary Capital Project of Chandigarh from 1948 to 1956. In this period he did outstanding work in the creation of the city of Chandigarh. Le Corbusier called him the 'Soul of Chandigarh.'

He served as Member union Public Commission from 1957 to 1962. For rendering very meritorious professional service, he was awarded the Padma Bhushan in 1974. He is the recipient of other coveted Indian/foreign awards including Member of the British Empire in 1938. In 1974 he was invited by the Tanzanian Government to advise them on their new Capital at Dadona. He was a very spiritual person. He expired in Chandigarh on 2 April 1995.

Rahul Mehrotra

Rahul Mehrotra is a practising architect and educator. He works in Mumbai and teaches at the Graduate School of Design at Harvard University, where he is Professor of Urban Design and a member of the steering committee of Harvard's South Asia Initiative.His practice, RMA Architects (www.RMAarchitects.com), founded in 1990, has executed a range of projects across India.

Mehrotra has written and lectured extensively on architecture, conservation and urban planning. He has written, co-authored and edited a vast repertoire of books on Mumbai, its urban history, its historic buildings, public spaces and planning processes.

Raj Rewal

A distinguished doyen of architecture from India, Raj Rewal is recognized internationally for buildings that respond with sensitivity to the complex demands of rapid urbanization, climate and culture.

Some of his creations include the Hall of Nations in Delhi; the Nehru Pavilion, Delhi; the Asian Games Village, Delhi; the Library for the Indian Parliament; the Lisbon Ismaili Centre, Portugal; the Indian Embassy in Beijing and the Visual Arts University, Rohtak.

Rewal has received many honours, including the gold medal for the Indian Institute of Architects, the Robert Mathew award from the

Commonwealth Association of Architects and Chevalier des Arts et des Lettres award from the French Government.

His works have been exhibited at the National Gallery of Modern Art, New Delhi and the Pompidou Museum, Paris.

Rajnish Wattas

Rajnish Wattas is the former principal of the Chandigarh College of Architecture and currently visiting professor at various institutions. Widely travelled, he has lectured at numerous prestigious forums in India and abroad, including Harvard University's Graduate School of Design and the Illinois Institute of Technology (IIT), Chicago. An architectural critic and authority on Chandigarh's modern heritage, he has focused on the city's landscape design considerably.

He has authored a huge compendium of professional writings and hundreds of general essays, travelogues and features in leading journals, newspapers and anthologies. He is co-author of two books, *Trees of Chandigarh* and *Sukhna—Sublime Lake of Chandigarh.* He has been a member on various expert groups including the one that evolved the 'Master Plan of Chandigarh–2031' and is currently member 'Chandigarh Heritage Committee'. He is a founder member of the Chandigarh Tree Lovers (CTL), a group that promotes awareness about Chandigarh's landscape.

S.D. Sharma

Ar. Shiv Datt Sharma has been associated with the 'Chandigarh Project' since the inception of the city from 1952 onwards. He has worked with architects Le Corbusier and Pierre Jeanneret on the Chandigarh project. S.D. Sharma was Chief Architect, Deptt. of Space, Government of India (I.S.R.O.), Bangalore from 1972 to 1979.

Besides many National awards, Ar. S.D. Sharma was awarded the Highest Honour of lifetime contribution in the field of Architecture 'IIA Baburao Mhatre Gold Medal 2001'. Many other prestigious awards are also associated with his firm. He was also awarded the prestigious 'Golden Architect Award A+D' and the 'Great Master's Award' by JK Cements. Actively involved in architectural practice he is designing many prestigious projects and is a part of the Chandigarh Heritage Conservation Committee.

Sumit Kaur

Starting her service with the Delhi Development Authority, she undertook various housing projects for different income groups in Delhi.

During her tenure in the Department of Architecture, Punjab, she designed prestigious projects such as District Administrative Complexes at Hoshiarpur and Moga, National Martyrs Memorial at Khatkar Kalan and Hussainiwala, State Judicial Academy, Chandigarh, etc.

While working in Department of Urban Planning, Chandigarh Administration as Chief Architect, she handled various educational, institutional, residential, landscape and commemorative projects.

She spearheaded the preparation of the Chandigarh Master Plan–2031, an exhaustive document providing vision for sustainable development. She also led the team in the preparation of the dossier of the Capitol Complex along with its management plan for inclusion in the Trans-national nomination submitted for UNESCO World Heritage status.

William J.R. Curtis

William J.R. Curtis is an award-winning historian, critic, painter and photographer. Educated at the Courtauld Institute and Harvard University, he has taught in many universities around the world including Harvard and the University of Cambridge where he was Slade Professor of Fine Art (2003–04).

His best known books include *Modern Architecture Since 1900* (3rd edition, Phaidon, 1996) and Le *Corbusier: Ideas and Forms* (2nd edition, Phaidon, 2015), both of which have been referred to as 'classics'. He contributes regularly to international critical journals such as the *Architectural Review and El Croquis* and is a fervent defender of modern architectural patrimony particularly in India. Currently a major retrospective of his artistic and photographic work is on show in the Alhambra, Granada with the title 'Abstraction and Light' (catalogue, TF Editores, Madrid, 2015). Among his numerous awards: a National Honors Society Gold Medal in Architecture and Allied Arts, USA (1999), a Medal of the Museum of Finnish Architecture (2006) and a Golden Award for Global Contribution in Architecture (CERA, A+D, India, 2014).

ACKNOWLEDGEMENTS

An anthology like *Le Corbusier Rediscovered: Chandigarh and beyond* with essays by 12 internationally reputed and diverse contributors is surely a huge team effort. However, our foremost gratitude is due to those, who firstly believed in the idea of this book and fully supported its publication. Therefore, our greatest gratitude is due to the Chandigarh Administration, headed by His Excellency Sh. V.P. Singh Badnore, Governor Punjab & Administrator U.T. Chandigarh. Going beyond just his Administration's support, he has been most kind in agreeing to write the Foreword for the publication also, thereby imparting it a special stature.

Similarly, without the support of Sh. Parimal Rai, IAS, Advisor to the Administrator this book would not be published. We're very grateful to Sh. Anurag Agarwal, IAS, Home-cum-Tourism Secretary, Chandigarh Administration, for immersing himself completely in the book project and preceding that of organizing the Symposium 'Celebrating Le Corbusier: 50 years after the Master' held in 2015 the raison d'être for this book to be born. An anthology like this frequently runs into rough weather and roadblocks, which were instantly resolved by Mr Agarwal's personal and passionate interventions to ensure the book project was realized. It was therefore unthinkable to realize this book without thanking him enough.

Thanks are also due to Ms Kavita Singh, IAS, former Director Tourism, for her pivotal role in coordinating the 2015 Symposium into a huge success— the core foundation of this book. The encouraging and supportive role of the present Director Tourism, Sh. Jitender Yadav, IAS, is gratefully acknowledged for his administrative support.

The book owes its existence to the enormous contribution of all the esteemed contributors, who took out their precious time and energy to write the various essays—not as mere texts of their presentations—but on our request especially written for the book, much after the Symposium. And they also very patiently responded to our numerous follow-up

Facing page:
Mill Owners Building,
Ahmedabad
© Deepika Gandhi

requests whether for additional/substitute images or suggestions or some modifications, etc. Therefore, this book owes its existence to the efforts of our iconic experts and is really the sum total of their collective contributions. We fall short of adequate words in thanking suitably Mr B.V. Doshi, Mr William J.R. Curtis, Mr Raj Rewal, Mr S.D. Sharma, Prof. Rahul Mehrotra, Mons. Michel Richard, Mons. Jacques Sbriglio, Prof Alfredo Brillembourg, Mr Jagan Shah and Ms Sumit Kaur. We thank William J.R. Curtis especially for his invaluable insights towards the layout and design of the book over and above the contributions of his essays.

Our heartfelt gratitude to the Fondation Le Corbusier for its prompt and generous permissions for using priceless images from its archives. We will also like to thank Mr Harish Khare, Editor-in-Chief of *The Tribune* for permitting us to use a key photograph from the newspaper's archives. Mr Suneet Paul, Editor-in-Chief of *Architecture + Design* was equally magnanimous in permitting us to reproduce an archival essay written by P.L. Varma, a rare publication. We're also grateful to the M.N. Sharma Architectural Foundation for allowing us to reproduce an essay by M.N. Sharma from the book *Making of Chandigarh: Le Corbusier and After.* Thanks are also due to Gen. Satinder Varma for contributing material on his father Mr P.L. Varma.

Gratitude is expressed for valuable help in the preparation of the manuscript to Shweta Sethi and Ishita Bhatnagar who undertook the painstaking work of transcription of the various presentations at the Symposium. Shweta also contributed to the finalization of images for the manuscript. Saanya Arora, Research Assistant, brought the book to life by preparing the first draft layouts and then patiently working on the numerous revisions thereof.

We acknowledge the support of our respective families which allowed us to invest our time and money in this architectural labour of love.

The editors of this book also whole-heartedly thank Niyogi Books Pvt Ltd and its dedicated team of editors and designers for their enthusiastic involvement, since the very start of the book project till its completion.

Rajnish Wattas
Deepika Gandhi

INDEX